CONSCIENTIAL ANTIWASTAGE

Evolutionary Choices in the *Age of Abundance*

Eliana Manfroi

CONSCIENTIAL ANTIWASTAGE

Evolutionary Choices in the *Age of Abundance*

Translation: Liliana Alexandre.

Foz do Iguaçu, PR
2019

Consciential Antiwastage – Evolutionary Choices in the Age of Abundance
Original title in Portuguese: Antidesperdício Consciencial – Escolhas Evolutivas
na Era da Fartura

Translation: Liliana Alexandre.

Revision: Jeffrey Lloyd.

Cover: Valesca Ferreira e Daniel Ronque.

Card Catalog Information

M276c	Manfroi, Eliana
	Consciential antiwastage : evolutionary choices in the Age of Abundance. / Eliana Manfroi ; translation: Liliana Alexandre ; [Preface Mabel Teles]. -- Foz do Iguaçu : Editares, 2019.
	256 p.
	Translation of: Antidesperdício consciencial : escolhas evolutivas na Era da Fartura.
	Includes bibliography.
	ISBN 978-85-8477-114-1
	1. Conscienciology. 2. Self-discernimentology. 3. Proexological self-planning. I. Alexandre, Liliana. II. Mabel Teles. III. Title.
	CDD 133

Tatiana Lopes CRB 9/1524

EDITARES INTERNATIONAL ASSOCIATION

Av. Felipe Wandscheer, 6200, sala 107, Cognópolis
Foz do Iguaçu, PR – Brasil – CEP 85856-530
Tel/Fax: +55 45 2102 1407

E-mail: editares@editares.org.br
Website: www.editares.org.br

Dedicated to my grandson Tommaso Vidor
Signori and to all consciousnesses being reborn in
these first decades of the XXI century. May they take
full advantage of the most overwhelming *Age of Abundance*
in evolutionary contributions to the History of Humankind.

ACKNOWLEDGEMENTS

Appreciation and memory always walk *hand in hand*, hence the importance of recording here my profound gratitude to the consciousnesses whose invaluable contributions enrich my present life. I wish to thank:

Professor Waldo Vieira *(in memoriam)*, Zephyrus, and his ultimate example of consciential antiwastage.

Mabel Teles, for her mentalsomatic *treat* in the form of a preface.

Valesca Ferreira, for the assistantial talent in being able to capture the full essence of my book in the cover design.

To the most excellent reviewers Milena Mascarenhas, Miriam Kunz, Ninarosa Manfroi, Roseli Oliveira, Sandro Batistella, Tatiana Lopes, Liege Trentin, Cathia Caporalli, Ivone Cubarenco, and Erotides Louly, my intellectual gratitude for your generosity, time, and knowledge, in helping me further qualify this book.

To editor Guilherme Kunz, and the teams at Editares and Epígrafe for the most important assistance one can offer a consciousness: help in the materialization of one's clarifying personal book.

To Fernando Barbaresco, my partner in our evolutionary duo, and *very rare friend*, my gratitude for everything.

To my parents Ricardo Manfroi *(in memoriam)* and Maria Lourdes Maschio Manfroi, sister Isabel Cristina Manfroi, and brother Paulo Ricardo Manfroi *(in memoriam),* for having been there for me in this lifetime, for your affection, and for providing me with so many opportunities to study, and always encouraging me to write.

To Pedro Manfroi Signori, my son and evolutionary friend from so many lives – you are living proof that I have not wasted the essential.

Eliana Manfroi

Index

SECTION III
ANTIWASTOLOGY

PREFACE

Authorial Stamina

Wisdom. *To know how to live productively* is the challenge imposed on every lucid human being. *Knowing how to live productively* in this *Age of Abundance*, i.e., in times where there is an excess of opportunities, stimuli, interactivity, entertainment and conveniences in present-day life, is paradoxically even more intriguing if we consider the ubiquitous waste in modern society.

Questioning. Crucial questions arise in this context. How can we evolutionarily use the diverse resources of contemporaneity? How can we avoid wasting time, energies, and consciential attributes on expendable continuously changing fads? What could we discard amongst the abundance of 21st century possibilities, in order to achieve a fruitful existence from an evolutionary point of view? How could we apply the contributions received in our current human life, avoiding consciential wastage, in search of complexis?

Background. These questions ground and guide the book the reader has in their hands, functioning as a reflection chamber and evolutionary alert for all conscins, and in particular those committed to making their current life a successful interassistantial proexological enterprise.

Relevance. Such desideratum makes the book *Consciential Antiwastage – Evolutionary Choices in an Age of Abundance* a highly relevant and priority work, as an antidote or prophylaxis to deviations in general, by realistically pointing out not only the details of the pathology itself, but principally the paths and techniques aiming for self-improvement.

Hypothesis. The researcher, journalist, and psychologist Eliana Manfroi starts from the hypothesis that among the megawastage of our present-times, the condition of self-wastage stands out, meaning, the act of the wasteful individual wasting themselves, neglecting existential contributions, strongtraits, and evolutionary resources. Among the possible effects of this choice are living with the *consciential self-banalization syndrome,* in evolutionary mediocrity, stagnant paralysis (doldrumology), among others, causing in certain conditions an existential void, and further down the road leading to incomplexis.

Wastology. Given this premise, the author exemplifies the intricacies, comprehensiveness, and nefarious effects of *wastology,* based on an interdisciplinary approach, filled with clear factums capable of illustrating, in a practical and factual way the pathology under analysis.

Therapeuticology. In this therapeutic approach to the subject, the author inventories postures, guidelines, and techniques that can be applied by anyone interested in making qualified personal choices. In the midst of such proposals, the attentive reader will find the clarifying example of Eliana Manfroi herself, the first *confessed guinea-pig conscin* in this handbook, even though we are not looking at an autobiographic work here.

Conformatics. From the point of view of stylistics, the author's ability and technicality in using, in a timely manner, different language resources, imparting not only lightness and fluidity to the conformatics of the text, but above all qualifying the clarification sought and imprinting her *personal touch* on it, deserves particular mention. This reality makes us infer the hypothesis of being before an *ancient consciousness* in a graphothosenic harvest, showing her *authorial stamina* with great propriety in her first conscientiological book.

Recommendation. *Consciential Antiwastage* is recommended to all individuals willing to carve their personal choices, with a sincere commitment to improve practical self-discernment without any appeal to unscrupulous subterfuges and stagnant ego defence mechanisms. *What is not good is definitively not good!*

Mabel Teles
Cognopolis, Foz do Iguaçu, 11th of February 2017.

Introduction

> **Choices.** No reading conscin should
> forget that **books** immortalize wisdom as well
> as immense nonsense, thus demanding careful choices.[1]

Context. We have never enjoyed, in all our past human lives over the millennia, so many opportunities and contributions converging on the acceleration of our own evolution. At no time, as at the beginning of the 21st century, did we receive so many resources and unavoidable invitations to the process of personal and consequently collective improvement as a species. However, the paradoxical fact is that, in the full validity of the *Age of Opportunity,* we also live in the *Age of Wastage.*

Megawastage. The excess of resources available to a significant percentage of humanity has stimulated a process antipodal to the hypersufficiency of people's livelihoods: the megawastages of contemporaneity.

Thesis. The main thesis, resulting from research carried out by the author, is that of self-wastage; the consciousness wasting itself amidst

---

1 **Vieira;** Waldo. *Léxico de Ortopensatas* (**Lexicon of Orthopensatas**); Foz do Iguaçu, PR; *EDITARES;* 2014; p. 616.

the abundance of all types of evolutionary contributions. The most relevant of these contributions, from the perspective of this book, is the fact that we are contemporaries, and some of us are even protagonists, of a neoscience – Conscientiology.

Positioning. Therefore, this book approaches the consciential self--wastage theme under the focus of a new paradigm, that of conscientiology, the neoscience proposed by Brazilian researcher, physician, and writer Waldo Vieira (1932–2015).

Complexity. Interdisciplinarity is highly valued in this study, despite the fact that the approaches presented by psychology, sociology, and anthropology, among other relevant sciences, do not yet comprehend consciousness to the same breadth and complexity as the consciential paradigm.

Model. The consciential paradigm makes explicit the reality of the entire consciousness being a self-lucid principle involved in a process of ongoing improvement. Through continual existences, in different dimensions and successive human personalities living singular experiences, each consciousness builds up their very own evolutionary trajectory. Achieving full maturity, self-discernment, and gradually becoming more useful for the evolution of other consciousnesses are the main objectives of this existential path, which has already lasted countless millennia, and we still do not know when it will end.

Bewilderment. In the *Age of Abundance,* an excess of stimuli and possibilities has led to greater disorientation and less frequent lucid use of opportunities. However, it only makes sense to study a problem if it is to seek solutions.

Challenges. *Seize the opportunities. Value the contributions. Prioritize the good of all. Choose what is essential. Give up on the superfluous.*

Decide with lucidity. How can we meet all these demands at a time when much of humanity feels confused and aimless about their own evolutionary choices?

Alert. Thinking about these challenges and reflecting on the relevance of lucidity and maturity in recognizing, valuing, and prioritizing such aspects, even in initial existential decisions, becomes unavoidable.

Author. In writing this text, the author´s proposal is to remind you, readers from all age groups, of such individual and personal commitment to self-evolution, just as she would have liked to have found a similar warning early in adulthood. *Forewarned is forearmed.*

Self-experience. The author´s interest in studying and writing about this theme – consciential antiwastage – arose from her personal history. While reflecting about proevolutionary contributions received since infancy, and the intimate notion that her current life brought her the opportunity to *turn the table* evolutionary speaking, when compared with past existences, the conclusion was that a considerable percentage of opportunities, evolutive partnerships, and personal talents had been squandered, hence the responsibility of sharing with other individuals personal reflections and experiences on this theme.

Autobiographic. Although this is not an autobiographic book, the author´s experiences regarding consciential antiwastage intersect with the proposed approaches and ideas. The synthesis of the research, reflections, and techniques developed to reverse the picture of self-wastage are shared here with readers, as are contributions by other consciousness researchers and thinkers referenced in the bibliography.

Antivictimization. It is far from the objectives of this book to stimulate the reader´s victimization and guilt. The goal is to alert and propose necessary self-reflection, self-assessment, and prophylactic and therapeutic techniques to be applied when confronting the *Self-wastage Syndrome,* many of which have been used by this author.

Cycle. Even so, this text is not only recommended for young consciousnesses, those faced with their first choices in life, but it is recommended to anyone facing the challenges of self-evolution and personal recycling at any stage of their life cycle.

Public. As a *first-aid handbook* concerning consciential antiwastage, this book is dedicated to all intermissivists, as well as to all consciousnesses determined to qualitatively advance towards self-evolution. The author intends to be an attentive reader of the ideas contained herein, in a future existence.

Intermission. Intermissivists are consciousnesses reborn on this planet that had the opportunity to study and plan their current lifetime, with the assistance of evolutionary technicians, in order to make the best possible use of this new opportunity to live in this dimension. In short, those consciousnesses who have come better prepared to assist Humanity, due to their personal traits and the baggage of their experiences from previous lives. This book is dedicated to these consciousnesses, in the manner of an *Intermissivist's Handbook.*

Handbook. This *Intermissivist's Handbook* consists of a set of techniques, procedures, resources, guidelines, postures, and avoidances capable of contributing to the attainment of existential completism, for the use of the intraphysical consciousness coming out of a preresomatic course, as a *vade-mecum* of one's personal life-project (See **Manfroi,** Eliana; *Intermissivist Handbook;* encyclopaedia verbet; In: **Vieira,** Waldo; Org.; *Encyclopaedia* *of Conscientiology;* defended at the *CEAEC's Tertuliarium,* Foz do Iguaçu, PR, on 09.10.2015)[2].

Notebook. During the reading of this book, we recommend you always keep a self-research notebook at hand, so you can make notes based on gradual self-diagnosis, self-reflections, and application of suggested techniques.

Structure. This book is organized into 3 sections, each of them a speciality of conscientiology, and 21 chapters. Each chapter begins with an aphorism, *pensata,* or *maxim* pertinent to the theme, created by the excellent lexicologist Dr. Waldo Vieira. The *maxims* cited in this work are from the book *Léxico de Ortopensatas* (Lexicon of Orthopensatas), by the referred lexicographer, published in 2014.

Phrases. At the end of each chapter, the reader less familiar with conscientiological publications will find a *synthesis* of the chapter's *content,* in the form of an *emphatic phrase,* a technique also devised by Dr. Vieira.

Excesses. In the first section of this book – under ***Abundanceology*** (the science of abundance), the reader will find arguments related to the fact that our current state of abundance, never previously experienced, may generate a *paradox: excess of opportunities – risk of waste.* This section also presents the conscientiologic concepts of existential program and existential provisions as windows of opportunity, and one's consequent responsibility in repaying such contributions.

---

2 *Encyclopaedia of Conscientiology* entries, or *verbets* defended at CEAEC's – *Centre for the Higher Studies of Conscientiology – Tertuliarium,* in Foz do Iguaçu, Parana, Brazil, until now not yet published electronically or in print (Base date: February 2017), will be referenced in this manner throughout the book, and can be accessed at the following site:<www.tertuliaconscienciologia.org>.

Sense. Also in the first part of the book, the *sense of evolutionary usefulness* manifested by numerous consciousnesses, particularly intermissivists who have technically prepared themselves during the so-called *intermissive period* (the interval between one life and the next, in the extraphysical dimension) is discussed. In addition, the author proposes 2 techniques she applied: the *existential self-audit technique* and the *ambitionlessness technique*.

Criticality. Closing section I, the author presents an argumentative proposition about the current human existence being hypercritical in nature, meaning, it representing a *parting of the waters*, and a *game changer* regarding personal evolution.

Pathologies. In section II of the book – **Wastology** (the science of waste), facts and arguments are presented to support the observation that we are also living, concomitantly, amongst abundance, in an *Age of Wastage*. This leads to pathologies of excess and to self-wastage syndromes. An example of the effect of such disorders is the experience of the epidemic so-called *existential void,* a theme we explore in depth in the chapter of the same name. In order to assist the reader in their self-reflections, some types of self-wastage are presented, their stagnating consequences, and their onus on personal evolution also considered.

Antiwastage. The third and last part of this book – **Antiwastology** (the science of therapeutics and prophylaxis against waste) brings arguments supporting the hypothesis that we may be living, in the 21st century, even if paradoxically, an *Age of Lucidity,* despite all the disorientation and lack of discernment.

Overcome. Also proposed are techniques for the prevention and overcoming of self-wastage, amplified by complementary analyses, such as the avoidance of self-obsolescence, the need for evolutionary but also prudent audacity, and the price to be paid for daring to be *different* before the alienating flow of the still pathological intraphysical society.

Legaciology. To end the last section of the book, the ideas proposed are pertinent as regards the priority choices and the existential legacy of evolutionary values each reader will leave for themselves and their future lives on this planet.

Annex. The insertion of an entry, or *verbet*, published by the author in the *Encyclopaedia of Conscientiology*,[3] with a theme directly related to the essence of this work, can be found as suggested complementary reading.

Disbeliefology. The readers are emphatically invited to read Dr Vieira´s *pensata* opening this introduction and to maintain, throughout the reading of this book, their critical sense and discernment as regards the ideas presented herein. In conscientiology, a corner stone for all of us is the ***Principle of Disbelief,*** present in every approach of this new science: ***Do not believe in anything, not even in the information presented in this book. Perform your own research and have your own experiences on the theme proposed.*** The author would therefore kindly ask you to subject all ideas presented in this book to contemplation, analysis, and reflection before reaching conclusions, in the expectation that you draw your conclusions from your own personal experience. It is sincerely hoped that by the end of your reading, you can find that your precious time has not been wasted.

The author
Cognopolis Foz do Iguaçu, February 2017
Email: elianamanfroi@gmail.com

---

3 The *Encyclopaedia of Conscientiology* is a collective work that has been created by several hundred co-authors, each a conscientiology researcher, under the coordination of Dr Waldo Vieira, until 2015. After this date, its coordination and production is the responsibility of ENCYCLOSSAPIENS – *the International Association of Conscientiologic Encyclopaediology.*

SECTION I
ABUNDANCEOLOGY

1. The Age of Abundance

Achievements. No matter how great a thing done in the past, it is small when compared to what you can **achieve today,** particularly considering our current *Age of Abundance and technological development.*[4]

Definition. *The Age of Abundance* is the historical era or period of time, hypothetically iniciated in the second half of the 21ˢᵗ century, characterized by the availability of an abundance of all kinds of resources, contributions, inputs, goods, and subsidies to the human population.

Synonyms: 1. *Age of Wealth.* 2. *Age of Prosperity.* 3. *Age of Plenty.* 4. *Cycle of Plenty.*

Antonyms: 1. *Age of Scarcity.* 2. *Age of Indigence.* 3. *Cycle of Poverty.* 4. *Age of Penury.* 5. *Age of Wastage.*

Post-war. With the end of World War II in 1945, there was a period of optimism in the countries who won the war and world economic growth resumed, with the large-scale production of accessible material goods. In the United States alone, during the post-war period, millions of babies were born in a population boom known as the *baby boomer generation.*

---

4 **Vieira,** Waldo; ***Léxico de Ortopensatas*** (**Lexicon of Orthopensatas**); Foz do Iguaçu, PR; *EDITARES;* 2014; p. 1.423.

Millennium. At the end of the 20th century, and entering the 3rd millennium, planet earth is already overpopulated and the *abundance industry* feeds a new generation of ravenous consumers.

Abundance. In this second decade of the 21st century, we live in an *Age of Abundance* of opportunities and contributions, both material and intellectual, albeit unequally distributed among Humanity. Never before in history have human beings had so many ways to change themselves and their societies for the better.

Accumulation. Our immense technological advancements, though helpful, have not so far solved the critical civilizing issue of consciential evolution. Maturescence of the consciousness and the ethical and cosmoethical aspects involved in the planetary evolutionary mechanism has not accompanied the cutting-edge technology. We have been accumulating gigantic scientific, technical, intraphysical, and intellectual knowledge, but in contrast, intraconsciential improvement and expansion of fraternal conviviality to the whole planet is not yet a reality.

Innovation. When attentively looking at the multimillenary civilizational process, we observe this abundance is a recent fact in our history.

Freedom. Periods of extreme scarcity of resources of all kinds, such as food, health, security, energy, peace, and above all freedom of expression, have permeated most of our human trajectory on this planet. There were periods of the civilizing process, such as during wars, in which eating once a day was considered a privilege, and having a spare garment to wear almost a luxury. Little more than 4 centuries ago, being able to read and write were the skills of a privileged few, generally the clergy, nobility, and intellectualized aristocracy (See **Fischer**, Steven; *História da Leitura* (**A History of Reading**); São Paulo, SP; *Editora UNESP*; 2006, p. 206).

Health. While improvements in the quality of life today may seem banal, improvements such as "simple" potable water piped to homes guaranteed health and avoided devastating infectious diseases. Drinking water without the worry of potentially dying of cholera within the next 48 hours is a certain relief. Just over four thousand years ago, seeking food and security occupied almost all of the time and energy of the short life of our distant ancestors.

Lighting. Another basic example of past restrictions was that for many centuries the absence of artificial light made intellectual and manual work a lot more strenuous. During the winter months the sun would set around 5pm followed by at least 15 hours of darkness until morning. Candles were insufficient to illuminate rooms and allow reading, writing, and other productive activities. (See **Johnson**, Steven; ***Como Chegamos até aqui: A História das Inovações que Fizeram a Vida Moderna Possível* (How We Got to Now: Six Innovations That Made The Modern World)**; Rio de Janeiro, RJ; *Zahar;* 2015; p. 165 and 166).

Cost. The actual price paid for energy today is much lower than at the beginning of 19th century, for example, when the cost of a single tallow candle amounted to 6 hours of labour. In England, around 1300, artificial light was twenty thousand times dearer than today (See **Diamandis**, Peter; & **Kotler**, Steven; ***Abundância: O Futuro é Melhor do que Você Imagina* (Abundance: The Future Is Better Than You Think)**; São Paulo, SP; *HSM Editora;* 2012, p. 58 and 59).

Information. Books, for example, were so expensive and rare in the Middle Ages (5th to 15th century) that stealing one could lead the offender to the death penalty. It would have been possible to spend a lifetime in medieval times without ever seeing a single book. It therefore becomes pointless to argue against the profusion of books in contemporary editorial *Abundanceland.*

Libraries. In the 14th century, only around 200 school books were circulating throughout Paris, France (See **Fischer,** Steven; *História da Leitura* (**A History of Reading**); São Paulo, SP; *Editora UNESP;* 2006, p. 74). How was the situation in other cities of Europe, where publishing was apparently even scarcer? Probably worse.

Knowledge. Considering that knowledge materialized in the form of books is also recent and they have never been so bountiful, one can see the importance of using well our access to advanced cognition.

History. An English historian and book specialist, Martyn Lyons (1946–), analysed the existence of textual communication in human history by proposing an analogy with the 12-month calendar of a single year. The beginning of writing, in Summer, would correspond to the first day of January, the codex (texts in book format as we know them to-day) were invented in September of that same year. Johannes Gutenberg (1398–1468) would have made his first print at the end of November. In turn the *internet* showed up noon on the 31st of December, and *e-books,* in the evening of the last day of the year. Lyons affirms that we are living in the first *Information Society* in history (See **Lyons,** Martyn; ***Livro: Uma História Viva*** (**Books: A Living History**); São Paulo, SP: *Editora SENAC;* 2011, p. 11).

Speed. Brazilian writer Gabriel Perissé (1962–) proposes, in a creative way, in his preface to the book *Como Educar sua Mente* (apud Bauer, 2015, p. 11), that we are just in the "Middle Ages", even at the dizzying speed of information we have now and the risk of dispersion due to the excess (See **Bauer,** Susan Wise; ***Como Educar sua Mente: o Guia para Ler e Entender os Grandes Autores*** (**How to Educate your Mind: a guide for reading and understanding the great authors**); pref. Gabriel Perissé; São Paulo, SP: *É Realizações;* 2015, p. 11).

Supercommunication. The volume of available information is perhaps one of the main characteristics of our current *Age of Abundance.* Probably one single edition of a big newspaper like the *New York Times,* for instance, contains more information than one single common person could have accessed during their entire life in 17th century England (See **Veja;** *A Angústia do Excesso de Informação* (**information overload angst**); magazine; São Paulo, SP: *Editora Abril;* 05.09.2001; p. 62 to 66).

Information. Diamandis and Kotler (2012) reveal that, until 2003, humanity had produced 5 exabytes of digital information (1 Exabyte equals 1 billion gigabytes). However, in 2010 humankind was already producing 5 exabytes of information every 2 days. In 2013, the estimate was the generation of the same quantity of exabytes every 10 minutes (See **Diamandis,** Peter; & **Kotler,** Steven; *Abundância: O Futuro é Melhor do que Você Imagina* (**Abundance: The Future Is Better Than You Think**); São Paulo, SP; *HSM Editora;* 2012, p. 51).

Dispersion. If, on the one hand, the abundance of information facilitates access to knowledge, it can paradoxically create a poverty of attention, a dispersion trap, and an absence of focus, the antechambers to self-wastage.

Population. At the end of the 17th century, the world population was estimated at 600 million inhabitants. Just over 2 centuries later, in the 1950s of the post-war period, the world population had already reached 2.5 billion resomated consciousnesses. In just 65 years, this number jumped to 7 billion (2015).

Demographics. The UN report *World Population Prospects: The 2015 Revision* indicates it is possible that by 2050 Earth will be home to 9.7 billion inhabitants. By 2100, the same report estimates, 11 billion human beings will be living on the planet (See *United Nations, Department of*

Economic and Social Affairs, Population Division (2015). World Population Prospects: The 2015 Revision, New York, 2015; p. 1).

Challenge. The intraphysical challenge in the second half of the 21st century is to ensure clean water, healthy food, housing, quality education, health care, and clean non-polluting renewable energies for almost 10 billion people.

Megachallenge. However, the multidimensional megachallenge will be to ensure the extraphysical population of, hypothetically, at least another 60 billion consciousnesses, the right of access to evolution. Vieira estimated this figure (2007) upon considering the existence of 9 extraphysical consciousnesses for each intraphysical one (See **Vieira**, Waldo; ***Homo sapiens pacificus;*** Foz do Iguaçu, PR: *CEAEC – International Association for the Higher Studies in Conscientiology; & Editares International Association;* 2007; p. 946).

Brains. Italian sociologist Domenico de Masi (1938–) reminds us that when we talk about a demographic explosion, the first idea that springs to mind is the number of mouths to feed, without considering that each mouth has a brain attached to it. For him, 7 billion brains wake up every morning and start thinking, "representing the most voluminous brain mass ever seen on the planet, capable of creating big problems, but even more capable of finding great solutions" (See **Masi**, Domenico de; ***O Futuro Chegou: Modelos de Vida para uma Sociedade Desorientada*** (**The Future Has Arrived: Lifestyles for a Disorientated Society**); Rio de Janeiro, RJ: *Quitanda Cultural & Casa da Palavra;* 2014; p. 364).

Longevity. Masi (2014) also compiled the crescendo of humanity's average life expectancy across history: 29 years for the Neanderthals; 36 in Pericles' Athens; 45 during Napoleon's time; 47 in 1900, and 80 years of age by 2000.

Facts. The fact is that even with misery and hunger devastating entire populations, the vast majority of humanity is better fed, sheltered, protected from disease, and more likely to live to old age than their ancestors.

Availability. In the last 200 years, availability of almost everything a person could ever wish for has been increasing, including: life expectancy, hours of privacy, faster means of travel, more efficient means of communication, and more opportunities of all kinds. Diamandis and Kotler (2012) estimate that even admitting the hundreds of millions still living in deprivation, the current generation of human beings has access to more calories, watts, lumens-hour, square meters, gigabytes, distances travelled in less time, and financial resources than any previous generation (See **Diamandis**, Peter; & **Kotler**, Steven; *Abundância: O Futuro é Melhor do que Você Imagina* (**Abundance: The Future Is Better Than You Think**); São Paulo, SP; *HSM Editora;* 2012, p. 60).

Indicator. Nowadays we live longer and more productive lives. Among the many consequences of the improved conditions of our intraphysical lives is our increased longevity, this is most notable from the 20th century onwards. This is the surest indicator of the current abundance in terms of productive years we can dedicate to evolution.

Rebirths. Throughout many rebirths along human history, there were rare chances to attain longevity, productive maturity, and wisdom derived from the experience a long life brings, as we have in the current *Age of Abundance.* To be born and live long enough to be able to make life itself useful was the privilege of only a few.

Supercentenarians. Research has announced that the man or woman who will live to 150 years of age, with preserved mental attributes, has already been born. We now live longer in the intraphysical dimension than in our previous lives, with the opportunity for a greater existential yield.

Questioning. What have we been doing with this abundance and all these extra years to live? Evolving would be the most intelligent answer. But are we really making the best of this opportunity?

Return. For Vieira (2014, p. 107), our current human lives in the 21st century, are equal, in terms of opportunities and evolutionary performance, to the past 15 lives put together. That is, this present life can yield, evolutionary speaking, as much or even more than 15 lives in prior centuries, cultures, and personalities.

Amplification. Considering this ratio from *evolutionary mathematics*, the author warns us of the fact that 1 mistake committed in our current lifetime corresponds to 15 past mistakes, and that existential failure today equates to 15 past failures. In short, a single present act of self-wastage equals 15 wasted opportunities in retroexistences (See **Vieira, Waldo**; ***Dicionário de Argumentos da Conscienciologia* (Dictionary of Conscientiology Arguments)**; Foz do Iguaçu, PR: *EDITARES*; 2014; p. 107).

Appreciation. Why is human life so valued today? Among other causes, the author indicates the advanced self-awareness already reached by consciousnesses that have participated in existential training to prepare for their current resoma, the so-called *Intermissive Course,* the mega-contribution to this *Age of Abundance of Evolutionary Opportunities.*

Freedom. Another evidence for such a valuation is that there is no record in human history of the current level of freedom of expression regarding leading edge ideas on the essence of the evolutionary process, and the conditions for the lucid good application of such abundance.

Revolution. The present difficulty lies, inversely, in selecting, in the face of abundance of all sorts of ideas and material panacea, those of an evolutionary nature. An example of this freedom is the proposal of a conscientiological revolution, and the leading edge relative truths conscientiology's new paradigm presents, over the last two decades of the 20th century and until today.

Intermissiology. One of conscientiology's fundamental principles is multiexistentiality (successive lives). The technical preparation a consciousness does for an upcoming rebirth in a new soma (resoma) is called the *intermissive course,* this being a basilar factor of the future life's project – the *existential program* (proexis) of an *intraphysical consciousness* (conscin). Those who participated in this training in the period between lives, while still extraphysical consciousnesses (consciexes), and are now resomated are called *intermissivists.*

Challengeology. The megachallenges of humanity at the beginning of the third millennium are not only focused on solving intraphysical demands, be they geopolitical, economic, and social, but are primarily centred on the qualitative turning of the evolutionary threshold of most intra and extraphysical consciousnesses linked to this planet.

Reurbanization. While in the physical dimension, world leaders are dealing with problems such as the planetary demographic explosion, armed conflicts, and climate change, extraphysically, in the midst of the *Age of Reurbanization,* the priority task force works on the improvement of all dimensions, considering the parapopulation of consciousnesses still lacking evolutionarily, which goes far beyond mere material demands.

Definition. Reurbex is "a change for the better of unhealthy, anticosmoethically deteriorated extraphysical environments and communities that is sponsored by *Serenissimi*,[5] envisaging the sanitization of the

---

5 *Serenissimus* is the denomination indicated by Vieira (2007, p. 908) for the consciousness with a high level of evolution, anonymously working for the evolution of Humanity.

intraphysical holothosene of entire areas of the Socin where deleterious evolutionary influences are still exerted on humanity" (See **Waldo**, Vieira; *Homo sapiens reurbanisatus;* Foz do Iguaçu, PR: *CEAEC;* 2004, p. 245).

Acceleration. Since the 1940s, the reurbex has been accelerating with the resoma of a large number of intermissivists, and also with the rebirth of a significant contingent of reurbanized consciousnesses, those truly evolutionary disadvantaged, beyond material needs.

Consreus. A reurbanized consciousness is the man or woman that due to pathological processes of their manifestation during successive lives stayed a long time without being reborn, in some cases even centuries, stagnated in degraded extraphysical environments, in the generically called baratroposphere (*hell,* in the interpretation of Catholicism, and *umbra,* for Spiritists).

Strength. Earth's reurbanization has been prepared for centuries, gaining extra strength in the second half of the 20th century, and right after the end of World War II (See **Waldo**, Vieira; *Homo sapiens reurbanisatus;* Foz do Iguaçu, PR: *CEAEC;* 2004, p. 265).

Recycling. One of the main objectives of reurbanization is to promote the recycling of intraphysical human communities intruded by degraded extraphysical ones, this being largely the cause of critical issues, such as unbridled demographic explosion and overcrowding in this human dimension (See **Vieira**, Waldo; *Homo sapiens reurbanisatus;* Foz do Iguaçu, PR: *CEAEC;* 2004, p. 247).

Interassistantiality. The high number of reurbanized consciousnesses being reborn, lacking any kind of reeducation is, paradoxically, the unique opportunity to perform one of the best practices to optimize personal and group evolution: lucid interassistance to these consciousnesses through clarification as regarding the essential realities of the cosmos. *The greatest need of humankind is evolution.*

Zeitgeist. It is worth reflecting on 38 nuances of the diversity of the *zeitgeist* listed here in alphabetic order, the *ages* coexisting at the beginning of the 21ˢᵗ century, the evolutionary scene of billions of consciousnesses:

01. *The Age of Abundance of Consciential Energies.*

02. *The Age of Celebrities.*

03. *The Age of Clarification.*

04. *The Age of Cognitive Hyperstimulation.*

05. *The Age of Consciential Obscurantism.*

06. *The Age of Conscientiology.*

07. *The Age of Cosmoethics.*

08. *The Age of Empathy.*

09. *The Age of Fraternity.*

10. *The Age of Glasnost.*

11. *The Age of Generalized Anxiety.*

12. *The Age of Globalization.*

13. *The Age of Hyperconsumerism.*

14. *The Age of Hyperindividualism.*

15. *The Age of Intraphysical Recycling.*

16. *The Age of Lucidity.*

17. *The Age of Omninformation.*

18. *The Age of Partnership.*

19. *The Age of Peace.*

20. *The Age of Acceleration of Personal History.*

21. *The Age of Resentment* (book by Luiz Felipe Pondé, 1959–).

22. *The Age of Reurbanized Consciousnesses* (consreus).

23. *The Age of Reurbex.*

24. *The Age of Scanning.*

25. *The Age of Self-discernment.*

26. *The Age of Serenissimi.*

27. *The Age of Spectacularization.*

28. *The Age of Supercommunication.*

29. *The Age of the International Cosmoethical Conscientiological Community (ICCC).*

30. *The Age of Transnational Insecurity.*

31. *The Age of Transparency of one's Personal Life.*

32. *The Age of Uncertainty* (book by John Kenneth Galbraith, 1908–2006).

33. *The Age of Void* (Gilles Lipovetsky's book, 1944–).

34. *The Age of Wastage.*

35. *The Consciential Age.*

36. *The Digital Age.*

37. *The New Age.*

38. *The Postmodern Era.*

Universality. We are currently living the most interactive and universalistic lives ever, when compared to past lives, in which closedness, geographical isolation, and scarce interrelationships often prevailed. The abundance of opportunities to interact and expand our interconsciential contacts today reaches unimaginable levels.

Digressology. Given the abundance of scenarios favourable to a consciousness that plausibly could contribute to the realization of one's personal and group life project, now and in the future, the most serious risk for hesitant intermissivists is to fluctuate between dispersion of consciential efforts and/or decidophobia, which can engender self-wastage.

THE AGE OF ABUNDANCE CAN BE SYNTHESIZED BY THE CHINESE SAYING: THE SAME SITUATION CAN REPRESENT BOTH A "RISK" AND AN "OPPORTUNITY", DEPENDING ON THE LUCIDITY AND SELF-DISCERNMENT OF A CONSCIOUSNESS.

Self-questioning. Do you, reader, find it difficult to recycle and make personal changes in the face of all the abundant inputs present at the beginning of the 21st century? Have you thought about what it would be like to evolve in absolute scarcity, as in previous lives?

2. Abundance of Existential Inputs

> **Inputs.** The most problematic among proexological
> inputs is to know exactly what we have received
> for ourselves and what we have received to be
> distributed among our **evolutionary co-passengers.**[6]

Paradigm. The technical planning of the reader's current existence, as that of this book's author, is given the generic name existential program, and gains evolutionary technicalities and professionalism through the *Intermissive Course,* as referenced in the previous chapter. The resources for performing this life plan can be called of *evolutionary* or *existential inputs.* This chapter is intended as a warning to avoid the waste of such proevolutionary advantages.

Definition. A *life project* or *existential program* is the conscious act of designing a plan for the evolution of our own consciousness, favouring a vision of the whole of one's and other's evolutionary needs, and both the intra and extraconsciential resources available for its implementation (See **Vieira,** Waldo; ***Manual da Proéxis*** (**Existential Program Manual**); Rio de Janeiro, RJ: *IIPC;* 1998; p. 9).

---

6 **Vieira,** Waldo. ***Léxico de Ortopensatas*** (**Lexicon of Orthopensatas**); Foz do Iguaçu, PR: *EDITARES;* 2014; p. 108.

Synonyms: 1. Life goal. 2. Existential task. 3. Meaning of life. 4. Evolution's strategic plan.

Antonyms: 1. Life adrift. 2. Existential void. 3. Existential improvisation.

Planning. One's proexis consists of previously planned priority tasks, and uses the potentials, talents, abilities, attributes, innate ideas, and the consciousness' entire multiexistential baggage for its attainment. To the experiences gathered by the individual, life after life, in a self-inheritance mode beyond genetics, we call paragenetics.

Compatibility. A proexis is compatible with the temperament of the consciousness it is intended for, being both singular and feasible (See **Vieira;** Waldo; ***Manual da Proéxis*** **(Existential Program Manual)**; Rio de Janeiro, RJ: *IIPC;* 1998; p. 21).

Maxiproexis. When the evolutionary project is broad, comprehensive, and involving a large number of consciousnesses it is called a *maxiproexis.* These are collective *wholesale* evolutionary enterprises, and not only for a single person or a reduced number of individuals of a specific group.

Evolution. A consciousness presents, among many characteristics, that of evolution. As an intelligent principle, a consciousness self-promotes constant improvement and complexification. This evolutionary dynamic considers the evolutionary demands of each one of us.

Cycle. Consciousnesses are all part of an evolutionary cycle: every consciousness evolves; every action generated by a consciousness determines a corresponding reaction; nobody evolves alone (groupality), and we evolve, primarily, when we become useful to other people.

Needs. Similar to a company producing goods or services to meet the needs of the market, a consciousness and its life enterprise need to meet evolutionary needs. Thus, evolutionary products to meet these demands need to be made available, such as ideas, courses, books, and institutions.

Tasks. Performing evolutionary tasks requires prerequisites stemming from the evolutionary preparatory training for our current life, which took place in an *Intermissive Course*.

Abundanceology. In the current *Age of Abundance,* the supplies for one's evolutionary life, or the resources for the implementation of one's life program, are readily available and constitute the existential inputs or contributions received by each consciousness.

Definition. *Existential input* is any and every resource or contribution received by the conscin during their life, particularly those received during the preparatory phase of one's self-proexis, and they consist of useful tools, learnings, and favourable conditions for the best possible performance of one's designated interassistantial tasks (See **Loche,** Laênio; *Aporte Existencial* (**Existential Inputs**); verbet; In: **Vieira,** Waldo; Org.; *Encyclopaedia of* **Conscientiology;** Foz do Iguaçu, PR: *EDITARES/CEAEC;* 8th Ed. Electronic; 2013; p. 847 to 853).

Preparatory. The preparatory phase for the implementation of one's proexis is the one that goes from birth to the age of 35, on average, when a consciousness receives the building blocks of their existential program. After the age of 35, the executive phase begins, with its achievements and results (See **Vieira;** Waldo; *Manual da Proéxis* (**Proexis Manual**); Rio de Janeiro, RJ: *IIPC;* 1998; p. 56).

Self-inventory. To carry out the survey of one's received inputs in current life, we can use the technique of listing all contributions the consciousness has received since birth. For example, in functional order, here are 12 areas to be mapped out by the reader interested in accounting for the existential contributions received, followed by some indicators of the quality of these contributions. The reader may wish to make their own list:

01. **Birthplace:** ethnic origin; country; favourable culture.

02. **Nuclear family:** the quality of maternal cares; healthy familial friendliness.

03. **Genetic inheritance:** family lineage with healthy genetics.

04. **Informal education:** access to books; an appreciation for learning and knowledge within the household.

05. **Formal education:** access to qualified education; higher education; scholarships and grants; inspiring teachers; the development of polyglotism.

06. **Employment:** an assistantial profession, for instance, in the areas of education or health.

07. **Friendships:** productive relationships; fraternal friendships.

08. **Affective relations:** a balanced emotional and sexual life; enriching affection; interassistantial couple; *evolutionary duo* (evolutionary technique).

09. **Freedom of thought:** being able to express one's own ideas without repression; freedom of choice.

10. **Accumulation:** material assets received and accumulated, in the exact measure of one´s evolutionary needs.

11. **Health:** access to health care and adequate food.

12. **Support:** assistance in moments of need; favourable interventions in critical situations.

Expansion. A reader interested in expanding their self-inventory list may wish to read the *Encyclopaedia of Conscientiology*'s verbet *Técnica do Autoinventariograma* (Self-inventoriogram Technique), where Fonseca proposes 280 variables for the analysis of the next existence (See **Fonseca,** Djalma; *Técnica do Autoinventariograma* (self-inventoriogram technique); verbet; In: **Vieira,** Waldo; Org.; *Encyclopaedia of Conscientiology;* Foz do Iguaçu, PR: *EDITARES/CEAEC;* 8th Ed. Electronic; 2013; p. 10,380 to 10,387).

Convergence. It seems logical that existential inputs are compatible and convergent with a consciousness' existential program. Conducting a detailed survey of the contributions received helps to map the guiding lines of one's life project.

TYPES OF EVOLUTIONARY CONTRIBUTIONS

Diversity. Evolutionary contributions, or inputs are of diverse natures and aims. To relate and analyse them all would require a separate book. However, it is worth highlighting the following 5 types of existential aids essential to proevolutionary autonomy, as received by a considerable percentage of readers in this *Age of Abundance.* The selection of only 5 types is due to the particular importance of these contributions to recycling, the attainment of a complete existential program, and the full utilization of one's current critical life, which we will analyse in chapter 7.

1. Input: Freedom

Autonomy. Freedom of thought and expression is the free manifestation of a consciousness´ ideas and opinions without any restriction or kind of repression.

Reality. The absence of free thought and action may not be the reader´s present reality, but in various parts of the planet it is still imposed on many consciousnesses at the beginning of this 3rd Millennium.

Value. Hence, when considering this existential contribution one should reflect upon the fact that a consciousness can resomate and live in a family and social environment characterized by freedom.

Will. Daou (1956–) synthesizes the importance of the contribution of evolutionary autonomy in her concept of *freedom of will. Freedom of will* is the cosmoethical and irreplaceable condition of being able to think, feel, and act freely, in diverse existential circumstances, simple or complex, when faced with the possibilities of decisions, choices and directions, which are drivers or constrictors of evolution (See **Daou, Dulce; *Vontade: Consciência Inteira* (Will: Consciousness in its entirety);** Foz do Iguaçu, PR: *EDITARES;* 2014; p. 149).

History. As in the example of the previous chapter, using historiology to evaluate how much Humanity has advanced, albeit slowly, becomes necessary for the analysis of this proexological (or existential) contribution. Consider, by hypothesis, your own personal condition of having had past lives in different contexts, social roles, and historical periods.

Slavery. Enslavement of a consciousness by another is an ancient practice. In Greco-Roman Antiquity, the possession of slaves was accepted "naturally", including by illustrious *humanist* Greek philosophers and eminent Roman jurists. The slave trade off the coast of West Africa peaked in the 18th century and had lasted for a few hundred years before the complete abolition of such practice (See **Masi,** Domenico de; *O Futuro Chegou: Modelos de Vida para uma Sociedade Desorientada* (**The Future has Arrived: Models of Life for a Disorientated Society**); Rio de Janeiro, RJ: *Quitanda Cultural & Casa da Palavra;* 2014; p. 103 and 104).

Interprison. Perhaps a lucid consciousness should be more worried by the fact of having been a slave trader than a slave, due to the fact that freedom of other consciousnesses is curtailed, in the first case, by subjecting them to cruel treatment, even though the two conditions are equally nefarious. In both situations, the restriction of freedom and the coercion of the will left profound intrasciential and existential marks.

Present. Slave labour still exists in the 21st century, but it is lived with much more freedom than was experienced in any other period of human history.

Self-repression. Religions have also been considerably effective in brainwashing consciousnesses, and further restraining intrasciential freedom. Legions of individuals have not even been allowed to "think" critically about imposed dogmas. It is worth noting though that many individuals are still being consciencially *brainwashed* today, or still being slaves of their own beliefs and prejudices of a religious nature.

Ideas. Thinking differently, in a more advanced manner, and spreading innovative, libertarian ideas, especially via writing, was even dangerous just over 3 centuries ago. How many freethinkers were persecuted and murdered by the repressive mechanisms of the Roman Catholic Church, such as the Inquisition, and despotic monarchical absolutism?

Prohibition. The *Index Librorum Prohibitorum* (Index of Forbidden Books) has been in force for over 400 years (1557–1966). The anathema of heresy fell upon any ideological adversary of the powers that be, with many condemned to the bonfire simply for *thinking differently*. Not infrequently, the books went to the bonfire along with their authors.

Media. The consciousnesses that think and express themselves in a free manner still run the risk of being thrown into today's multimedia defamatory "bonfires".

Freedom. Never before has Humanity enjoyed so much freedom to talk, write, publish, and express their thoughts.

Junk. The same principle, however, holds true for the "mountain of junk" that is produced and launched every year on the global publishing market. This is a prophylactic caveat for the reader to enjoy their freedom to select and choose what they read.

Intraconscientiality. The greatest of freedoms is still that of thinking, in the intimacy of each consciousness already capable of intraconscential pacification so they can think and act freely.

2. Input: Disbeliefological

Antidogmatism. Following on from the previous item, perhaps one of the main inputs endorsed by the consciential paradigm in the 21st century is that of antidogmatism, notably through the *Principle of Disbelief,* which invites every lucid consciousness to renounce any nature of beliefs and blind faith. This principle recommends the use of your best rationality and discernment in the face of any ideas or relative truths presented to you.

Input. The disbeliefological input represents the opportunity for the consciousness in its current life to think on its own, without any cultural, religious, ideological, or political brainwashing, but just making use of judicious self-learning through personal experience.

Sceptic. Vieira summarizes the stance of the *cosmoethical-optimistic-sceptic* consciousness as a prophylaxis for any ideational and experiential clash. The quest is no longer one for absolute truth, but for the relative leading-edge idea of the current evolutionary moment (See **Vieira**, Waldo; *Partilha do Saber* (**Knowledge Sharing**); *verbet*; In: **Vieira**, Waldo; Org.; *Encyclopaedia of Conscientiology;* Foz do Iguaçu, PR: *EDITARES/CEAEC;* 8th Ed. Electronic; 2013; p. 8,258 to 8,261).

Inheritance. As an invitation to the reader, evaluate the following to the extent possible, for how many lives have legions of consciousnesses been "forced to swallow" absolute and preconceived truths, without any right to doubt or question them. Deconstruction of this system of dogmatization is still ongoing and is expected to continue for a few more centuries.

Desacralization. Even so, we are living in a *culture of desacralization,* understood as a set of individual and collective concepts, knowledge, and behaviour, centred on the *Principle of Disbelief* and the deconstruction of the multisecular mentality of something and/or someone being sacred, divine, unquestionable, and consequently dogmatic.

Typology. Here are 7 types of disbeliefological conditions, listed horizontally in the order of complexity of themes, already under way at the beginning of this 3rd millennium: *desacralization* of money; *desacralization* of sex; *desacralization* of the book; *desacralization* of knowledge; *desacralization* of parapsychism; *desacralization* of the desoma, and the *desacralization* of evolution.

Self-myth. It is important for lucid consciousnesses to deconstruct the *self-myth* that knowledge, enlightenment, books, and writing itself constitute *sacred* items, and only for a privileged few, hence the importance of disbeliefology as a fundamental contribution or input in our present resoma. Disbeliefology is the antidogmatic vaccine of self-inoculation that is to be continually applied by all free-thinkers and independent consciousness researchers.

3. Input: Intermissive

Definition. The *intermissive input* is a set of clarifying acquisitions regarding oneself and evolution. A consciousness receives this during their strategic preparation to yield the maximum evolutionary benefits during their current human life, obtained in the extraphysical period prior to their present intraphysical existence.

Novelty. It is worth reminding the reader that, in all Human History, it is rare to find a consciousness possessing a positive balance in relation to generosity and assistantiality from previous lives and hence invited to participate in an *Intermissive Course*, ergo the condition of this support, and the responsibility of an intermissivist reader conscin.

Sense. Perhaps the greatest legacy of the preresomatic course is the innate self-conceptualization and original ideas brought, notably regarding the evolutionary meaning of human life, and familiarity with the ideas of conscientiology's paradigm. This is the *sense of evolutionary utility* that will be further discussed in chapter 5.

Divide. The *Intermissive Course,* a turning point or divide in the consciousness' evolutionary trajectory, seals the current evolutionary existence as being more critical than those experienced over millennia.

Scolding. When entering the *Intermissive Course,* a consciousness may have a consciential shock, or *parareality shock,* when perceiving the personal evolutionary *gap* between the lucid and orthothosenic manifestation of the intermissive course *teachers* and their own, in such cases this is perceived as a kind of proevolutionary scolding.

Impactherapy. A *proevolutionary scolding* is the act or effect of an intra or extraphysical consciousness receiving a self and a heteroreprimand, warning, rebuke, scolding, telling-off, claritaskal cosmoethical impactherapeutic admonition (See **Manfroi,** Eliana; ***Esbregue Pró-Evolutivo* (Proevolutionary Scolding**); verbet; In: **Vieira,** Waldo; Org.; ***Encyclopaedia of Conscientiology;*** defended at the *CEAEC Tertuliarium,* Foz do Iguaçu, PR, on: 02.06.2014).

Clarification. In the way of a *slap on the wrist*, contact with one's own reality clarifies the consciousness on rights and wrongs from their past, helping the reeducation and personal planning of one's future human life. Self-clarified, an intermissivist can keep in mind one of the main legacies of the *Intermissive Course,* the theory and practice of the *clarification task* (claritask).

4. Input: Reeducational

Definition. *Reeducational input* is the paradoxical condition of a consciousness that does not receive certain existential benefits, such as financial, social, and family contributions, yet still takes advantage of this apparent *scarcity* to eradicate weaktraits from their own personal temperament. Such a condition may favour reeducation, the development of an iron-clad will, and self-determination aimed at overcoming apparently constrictive conditions.

Excess. An abundance of inputs may in some cases represent a frank probation for a consciousness, due to the risk of extreme ease generating demotivation and waste.

Paradox. Considering an individual's temperament and holobiography, an evolutionary contribution may, paradoxically, be the absence of a particular input. This condition enables a lucid individual to increase self-efforts, and value each evolutionary conquest, recomposing an otherwise probable return to the waste and idleness of past lives, given the benefits received in the current.

Resilience. Overcoming adverse situations that end up strengthening the individual and making he or she able to help other people with similar difficulties, from personal example, receives the name of exemplary resilience (See **Manfroi,** Eliana; ***Binômio Resiliência-Exemplarismo* (Resilience-Exemplarism Binomial)**; *verbet*; In: **Vieira,** Waldo; Org.; ***Encyclopaedia of Conscientiology;*** Foz do Iguaçu: *EDITARES/CEAEC;* 8th Ed. Electronic; 2013; p. 2,462 to 2,466).

Strategy. By developing personal strategies of coping with difficulties and self-limitations, sometimes even of a somatic nature, a resilient consciousness structures techniques that can be used by many individuals with similar difficulties.

5. Input: Authorial

Definition. The *authorial input* is the resource, contribution, subsidy, or incentive, of a diversified nature, obtained by the conscin, facilitator of qualified conscientiographic production, notably clarifying conscientiological articles, encyclopaedic entries, and books (**Manfroi,** Eliana; ***Aporte Autoral* (Authorial Input)**; *verbet*; In: **Vieira,** Waldo; Org.; ***Encyclopaedia of Conscientiology;*** defended at the *CEAEC Tertuliarium,* Foz do Iguaçu, PR, on: 21.05.2014).

Form. This input may be explicit, like an inheritance received through kinship ties, as in the case of a renowned news company, a well-reputed publishing house, or simply intellectual parents. It can also be implicit, as in the ability to write (as a strongtrait) developed in consecutive resomas as an author.

Self-inventoriology. What about you, reader, do you identify having received explicit authorial inputs in your current life? In order to aid your reflection, here are, in alphabetic order, 12 questions that can be applied to map the incentives received regarding intellectuality and useful writing:

01. **Assistance.** Are original inspirations and ideas common during your personal practice of writing?

02. **Education.** Have the schools you attended encouraged and valued high quality written self-expression, right from the initial school years?

03. **Familiarity.** Did your parents' home provide enriching dialogues and debates through conversation with intellectualized adults? Did your family value reading and writing?

04. **Family.** Did the closest family encourage reading and erudition, making a considerable quantity of books available since childhood?

05. **Friendships.** Did your closest friends, from an early age, prioritize reading, discussion of ideas, and writing, to the detriment of acting out their consciential basement[7]?

06. **Library.** Did your city have at least one public library with up-to-date collections, favouring research and writing?

07. **Paragenetics.** Has the taste for reading, studying, and writing manifested itself early, immediately after literacy, indicating a habit and/or ability developed in previous lives?

08. **Patronage.** Was the opportunity to study through public or private scholarships and awards a constant in your own academic curriculum?

---

7 Consciential basement: phase of infantile and adolescent manifestation characterized by the predominance of primitive weaktraits of the consciousness (V. **Vieira,** Waldo; *Porão Consciencial* (**Consciential basement**); *verbet*; In: **Vieira,** Waldo; Org.; *Encyclopaedia of Conscientiology;* Foz do Iguaçu, PR: *EDITARES / CEAEC;* 8th Ed. Electronic; 2013; p. 8,568 to 8,571).

09. **Preceptor.** Did your caregivers provide a trained preceptor to accompany you during your childhood and/or adolescence?

10. **Profession.** Did your personal choice of profession facilitate the contribution of pro-erudition and writing resources?

11. **Self-learning.** Were conventional academic curricula experienced as a student routinely supplanted by spontaneous self-learning?

12. **Synchronicity.** Did artefacts of knowledge, such as books on subjects of interest, easily reach you, as if they *fell on your hands?*

Books. The volume of books and opportunities to develop useful erudition and intellectuality received in contemporary times is the greatest of all Human History.

Wisdom. Wasting 30 centuries of wisdom and erudition recorded and accumulated in the books already produced on this planet through the "simple" fact of not reading is an incalculable loss. Being able to read, reflect, and write, and not put this proevolutionary trinomial into practice, can be indicative of infra-endowment in one's evolutionary quotient (evolutionary intelligence) (See **Guzzo, J. R.**; *Analfabetos Voluntários* (**Voluntary Illiterate**); *Veja;* São Paulo, SP: *Editora Abril;* 11.06.2014; p. 100 and 101).

Casuistry. As a self-example, in the condition, as per conscientiology, of a *guinea-pig consciousness,* here are 2 specific cases of authorial input directly related to the existential program of many consciousnesses, included among them this author, and focused on writing and intraconsciential communicability. Having received numerous contributions in the area of producing texts, this book represents a sincere attempt to correspond, at least in part, to these inputs.

1. **Bibliophile.** The case of Venezuelan researcher and writer Fernando Báez (1970–), an authority on the study of the destruction of

books and libraries throughout History, and a consultant to UNESCO, is exemplary (See **Báez,** Fernando; ***História Universal da Destruição dos Livros: das Tábuas Sumérias à Guerra do Iraque*** (**Universal History of Destruction of Books: from the Sumerian Tablets to the Iraq War**); Rio de Janeiro, RJ: *Ediouro;* 2006; p. 19 and 20). He gives us an interesting account in the introduction of his book, showing that his mother worked in a grocery shop all day and left him in the care of a cousin, a secretary at the public library of the small town where they lived. The author, still a child, spent his days among the book shelves, reporting that he discovered the value of books and reading, at the time the books were his only childhood friends.

Inheritance. When he was 19, he became a seller of encyclopaedias, and one day received a box of about 40 volumes from the postman, left as an inheritance to him by his deceased grandfather. Among these books was William Blades' (1824–1890) *Enemies of Books* (1888). Báez himself said that this book was the cornerstone of the theme to which he would dedicate his existence: the preservation of Humanity's cultural assets.

2. **Preceptorship.** The American Susan Wise Bauer (1968–) was schooled at home by her parents, and at 3 years old she could already read thanks to having her mother as a teacher (See **Bauer,** Susan Wise; ***Como Educar sua Mente: o Guia para Ler e Entender os Grandes Autores*** (**How to Educate your Mind: a guide for reading and understanding the great authors**); São Paulo, SP: *É Realizações Editora;* 2015; p. 11 to 506). At 5, she could read the educational material equivalent to 5th grade at local schools. Her father's books, she recounts, played a key role in her studies as a historian, librarian, writer, and editor at *Peace Hill Press,* which she owns.

Languages. Susan learned Latin at 10, and after that Greek, Hebrew, Aramaic, and Korean. By 2014, she had already published 18 books

(3 of them before her 16th anniversary) and had 4 children. Emphasizing the importance of classic education, she wrote a guide to reading the great writers of universal literature, encouraging as much as possible the intellectual advantage to be taken from the books.

Repayment. The more abundant the existential contributions received, the more responsibility one has to repay them. The simple fact of having been reborn in this dimension and period of civilization already constitutes a substantial contribution. Numerous other consciousnesses still await an opportunity to live on this orb in their search for reeducation.

Anti-idleness. Idle evolutionary contributions indicate an incautious consciousness' absence of coherence and discernment regarding the megaresponsibility placed in their hands, as evolutionary loans that need to be repaid.

Capital. Again, Daou (2014) sums it up in the concept of *consciential capitalization,* and the importance of making good assistantial and evolutionary use of our current abundance of inputs. "*Consciential capitalization* is the act or effect of a conscin taking advantage of their human life, by producing the maximum evolutionary income from the existential contributions received, the knowledge accrued, the attributes conquered, and their multiexistential baggage, through the use of a lucid, granite-like, and theorical will" (**Daou,** Dulce; ***Vontade: Consciência Inteira*** (**Will: Consciousness in its entirety**); Foz do Iguaçu, PR: *EDITARES;* 2014; p. 192).

Multiplication. The responsibility of the intermissivist consciousness, a depository of proevolutionary inputs, is not only to repay them, but also to cosmoethically multiply the existential capital and distribute the dividends.

Contributions **constitute sure indicators of the consciousness'** *self-responsibility* **in repaying what was received through interassistance.** **A** **tool received signals the** *proexical work.*

Self-questioning. Have you, reader, already catalogued the existential contributions, of every nature, received in your present resoma? Have you been taking advantage of the opportunities to apply these proevolutionary resources?

3. WINDOWS OF EVOLUTIONARY OPPORTUNITIES

> **Opportunities. Opportunities** arise when you least expect them, anytime, anywhere. We must be prepared. Life is a continuation of opportunities created by our own consciousness.[8]

Definition. A *window of opportunity* is a temporary opening, aperture, fissure, crevice in the consciousness' evolutionary *continuum*, favourable, opportune, and conducive to optimization, betterment, or prophylaxis of some aspect relevant to personal recycling and to the realization of the maximum percentage of one's own existential program (complexis) (See **Manfroi,** Eliana; *Janela de Oportunidade* (**Window of Opportunity**); *verbet*; In: **Vieira,** Waldo; Org.; *Encyclopaedia of Conscientiology;* defended at the *CEAEC Tertuliarium,* Foz do Iguaçu, PR, on: 10.11.2012).

Synonyms: 1. Proevolutionary aperture. 2. Proexological opportunity. 3. Line of evolutionary aperture. 4. Pro-complexis prophylactic fissure. 5. Window of existential inputs.

Antonyms: 1. Window of inopportunity. 2. Antievolutionary locking. 3. Antiproexological closedness. 4. Inconsequential spendthriftness.

---

8 **Vieira,** Waldo; *Léxico de Ortopensatas* (**Lexicon of Orthopensatas**); Foz do Iguaçu, PR: *EDITARES;* 2014; p. 1.175.

Economy. An *economy of Good* is a principle in conscientiology that recommends, among the many available benefits and opportunities, the most intelligent is to choose *the greater good,* the priority, and that which will better serve the largest number of people possible, at an enlarged scale (See **Vieira,** Waldo; ***700 Experimentos da Conscienciologia*** (**700 Conscientiology Experiments**); Rio de Janeiro, RJ: *IIPC – International Institute of Projectiology and Conscientiology;* 1994; p. 633).

Evils. On the other hand, an *economy of evils* indicates that, among diverse situations and unfavourable contexts, before which a choice must be made, the option falls to *the lesser evil,* or that which will harm the least possible number of people, considering the damage it may inevitably cause (See **Vieira,** Waldo; ***700 Experimentos da*** **Conscienciologia** (**700 Conscientiology Experiments**); Rio de Janeiro, RJ: *IIPC – International Institute of Projectiology and Conscientiology;* 1994; p. 632).

Paradox. Reflecting on these two concepts, the *abundance of evolutionary opportunities paradox* arises. We are living in a historical moment where the possibilities are so numerous that we need to use the *Principle of the Economy of Good.*

Abundanceology. In the *Age of Abundance,* choosing what *not to do* is as fundamental as deciding *what to do.* In face of an excess of offers, discerning the priority is our current challenge.

Cycle. The choice of the *greatest evolutionary good* has a large chance of depending, *a priori,* on the consciousness' lucidity and maybe even on the life cycle stage it finds itself in. The life cycle is the course of life from birth to desoma, encompassing in short: childhood; adolescence; post adolescence; adulthood; middle age; early old age, and old age.

Deferment. Even considering exceptions, a child generally tends to be impulsive and can seldom defer the immediate satisfaction of a desire for a qualified future gain.

Experiment. Classic research performed in the 1970s at Stanford University, referred to by Giannetti (1957–) and Goleman (1946–), reports of an experiment carried out with pre-school children, which were taken to a room where sweets were available to them. The researcher would tell the child that if they could wait for 15 minutes until he was back, they could get 2 candies, instead of just the 1 immediately available to the child. Many children did not manage to defer gratification by maintaining their self-control, and ate the immediately available candy, hence losing the opportunity to have a second one (See **Giannetti,** Eduardo; *O Valor do Amanhã* (**The Value of Tomorrow**); São Paulo, SP: *Companhia das Letras;* 2005; p. 89 e 90; **Goleman,** Daniel; *Foco: A Atenção e seu Papel Fundamental para o Sucesso* (**Focus: The Hidden Driver of Excellence**); Rio de Janeiro: *Objetiva;* 2014; p. 81 and 82).

Appraisal. Without the pretence to compare a candy to an *evolutionary good,* the children in the experiment could have picked the *Principle of the Economy of Good,* if they had shown patience, self-control, and focus on the end results. The dilemma was, according to Giannetti: *less now* or *more later?*

Youth. Young adults perform well in the Stanford experiment, perhaps because they were less interested in children's sweets. The "treats" of today's youth are of a different nature. However, traces of impulsiveness and overvaluing the present, due to the view of having *all the time in the world* (future) to take care of evolution, can lead to wasting opportunities available in the *here and now.* "Digital treats" may be more appealing to young conscins.

Time. Underestimating the future, attributing excessive value to what is only in the present, is called *temporal myopia* by Giannetti, which can lead to short term choices without consideration of the evolutionary or regressive consequences (See **Giannetti,** Eduardo; *O Valor do Amanhã* (**The Value of Tomorrow**); São Paulo, SP: *Companhia das Letras;* 2005; p. 174).

Overestimation. On the other hand, overestimation of the future constitutes *temporal hyperopia*. For the author of *The Value of Tomorrow*, only minding the future can make us waste current demands and lose the windows of opportunity open in the present. Striking a balance would be to act in the present (choosing what is prioritary) to reach a certain goal (proexis), with an eye on the future (consciential evolution).

Prioritization. The challenge of choosing what is a priority requires, initially, substantial self-awareness, self-research to know what are your interests, tendencies, affinities, and abilities. Nobody wishes to loose time with something that has nothing to do with them. Another variable of weight in personal choices lies in the discernment as regards one's own existential program, and which options converge with one's purpose of life.

Life. To live, that is, to be born in the physical dimension again, is the first window of opportunity for a consciousness in evolution, with the objective of *polishing and refining* itself, life after life. Rossa (2014) synthesizes this idea in her book *Oportunidade de Viver* (Opportunity to Live), showing that "the school of life aims at individual and collective improvement that is gradually conquered and potentialized when the conscin is alert to this possibility" (See **Rossa**, Dayane; ***Oportunidade de Viver*** (**Opportunity to Live**); Foz do Iguaçu, PR: *EDITARES;* 2014; p. 40).

Self-diagnosis. In this *Age of Abundance* opportunities are many and varied in nature. As an example, here are 10, listed in alphabetic order, with the objective of assisting the reader assess their own degree of good use of such proevolutionary openings:

01. **Authorial window of opportunity:** access to erudition and specialized advice from institutions and support groups to a lucid author. These days, every determined and well-organized person can write and publish a useful book.

02. **Claritaskal window of opportunity:** chance of being able to perform *surgical* clarifications, that is, of assisting another consciousness in understanding the root of a problem.

03. **Exemplary window of opportunity:** the timely opportunity to demonstrate, through a personal example, self-improvement and resilience in the face of an existential aggravation.

04. **Infiltration window of opportunity:** invitation to work in a degraded social and consciential environment, as a lucid infiltrator, favouring the development of self-abnegation and interassistance (one knows where one is, and what one needs to do to help).

05. **Intermissive window of opportunity:** possibility of having participated of the first structured *Intermissive Course* in the parahistory of humanity.

06. **Paraperceptiologic window of opportunity:** discerned use of humanities second nature, parapsychism, in all instances of life.

07. **Recinologic window of opportunity:** experience of the *zone of maximum discomfort,* meaning, the self-saturation of one's own incoherencies and immaturities leading to a personal recycling previously postponed for centuries.

08. **Retrocognitive window of opportunity:** field research of one's own past lives, facilitated by the possibility of international travel, visits to museums, libraries, cultural centres, ancient archaeological sites, films, and online databanks.

09. **Scientific window of opportunity:** increasingly easy access to the formation and development of scientists committed to ethical science and concerned with the wellbeing of humanity. Paradox: the same goes for science and scientists focused on the development of equipment of war.

10. **Welfare window of opportunity:** unexpected illness of a family member requiring continued assistance and care, but allowing the opportunity for reeducation of the assistant, and the promotion of reconciliations.

Tasks. Among relevant opportunities available to all intermissivist consciousnesses in the current *Age of Abundance,* is our opportunity to assist ourselves and others, through clarification, regarding realities prioritary to evolution. This is what we call of *clarification task* (claritask). To understand this construct, we need to compare it with another concept – that of the *consolation task* (consoltask) (See **Vieira,** Waldo; *Homo sapiens reurbanisatus;* Foz do Iguaçu, PR: *CEAEC – International Association of the Centre for the Higher Studies of Conscientiology;* 2003; p. 47).

Console. It is possible to assist needy individuals by simply providing them with what they lack, such as the malnourished when they receive food from charities, or even from healthcare agencies. It is also possible to offer money to someone in debt, without teaching them financial self-organization and a prophylaxis of economic deprivation. Apparently such nice and generous attitudes do not solve the demand of the hungry and the defaulter; they only temporarily *soften* the situation. The hunger and debt will return. This type of assistance is what we call *consolation task* (consoltask).

Clarify. In the *clarification task* (claritask), the strategy is to assist the consciousness see the reality themselves, in depth, understanding the root and origin of the difficulties, and the self-responsibility for having reached such a situation. The consciousness is also advised on the many strategies available to reverse by itself the unfavourable personal scenario. This reversal, the profound intraconsciential personal change receives the name of *exis*tential *recy*cling (recexis).

Need. Consoltask is better than no assistance at all. However, in the present evolutionary moment we, and particularly intermissivists, can already put the claritask before the consoltask. To console, when you could already clarify, can be a waste of opportunity to truly assist someone at a higher level.

School-Planet. Humanity can still be considered in the condition of being like in a *hospital,* full of evolutionary patients, but in a moment when we can perform a huge turn to become a large *school,* full of evolutionary learners.

Clarification. A lucid consciousness opts for clarification task, as an evolutionary megopportunity to understand where the solution lies. To console is to postpone the cure for our lack of evolution. To clarify is comparable to an inoculation against the *disease* of antievolutionary self-ignorance.

Price. However, not every opening of a proevolutionary window presents a "rosy" and "sunny" scenario. This analogy refers to the fact that sometimes the opportunity demands efforts to recycle traits of the consciousness' temperament and anachronistic personal habits. It can also demand letting go of personal requirements, whims, complaints, and secondary minutiae in view of the importance of the envisioned assistantial task.

WHILE HELPERS OPEN WINDOWS OF EVOLUTIONARY OPPORTUNITY, NOT ALWAYS ROSY, BUT WITH A LARGE INTERASSISTANTIAL HORIZON, AN UNWARY CONSCIN CLOSES DOORS WHEN WASTING EVOLUTIONARY INPUTS.

Self-questioning. What about you, reader, have windows of opportunity already been opened for you, so you can make your current resoma a turning point in evolutionary terms? What has been your response: launching yourself with discernment into challenges, or turning your back on the given existential opportunities to evolve?

4. Self-responsible Reciprocity

> **Conscientiographology** – Do you wish to reciprocate for the abundance of opportunities you have received in your current lifetime? Write confidently, putting your ego in service of mentalsomatic assistance.[9]

Definition. *Self-responsible reciprocity* is the act or effect of a consciousness answering for proevolutionary contributions, inputs, and gains they received, by means of recognition, gratitude, return of personal patrimony, and interassistance to others.

Synonyms: 1. Self-responsible return. 2. Personal reciprocity commitment. 3. Lucid repay. 4. Conscious compensation of contributions.

Antonyms: 1. Anti-donator irresponsibility. 2. Egocentric ingratitude. 3. Reciprocity default. 4. Negligence in the restitution of contributions.

Self-donatiology. The main idea behind this chapter can be synthesized by the *reception-donation binomial*. An intermissivist's responsibility for the contributions received is immense and repaying via actions, attitudes, and assistantial undertakings is a strategy to attend to

---

9 **Vieira,** Waldo. *Léxico de Ortopensatas* (**Lexicon of Orthopensatas**); Foz do Iguaçu, PR: *EDITARES;* 2014; p. 405.

this self-responsibility (See **Vieira**, Waldo; ***Dicionário de Argumentos da Conscienciologia*** (**Dictionary of Conscientiology Arguments**); Foz do Iguaçu, PR: *EDITARES*; 2014; p. 315).

Returnology. As a faithful depositary, a consciousness assumes the responsibility of putting in practice the *law of return,* insofar as it assented to the commitment of repaying the contributions received in the *intermissive course*. It is a personal principle within the framework of paraduty, meaning, the obligations that extrapolate any intraphysical human law in scope and complexity (paracompromise). It is the jurisprudence of universal evolutionary laws (paralaw), that will find consciousness at any moment and dimension in which it manifests itself. Failure to face this evolutionary maximechanism is a gross mistake.

Paraduty. *Paraduty* is the condition of a consciousness lucid regarding their commitments, norms, principles, and just, upright and straightforward paralaws, established with the self-aware development of personal evolution linked to the evolutionary group's evolution (See **Vieira**, Waldo; ***Paradever*** (**Paraduty**); Org.; ***Encyclopaedia of Conscientiology;*** Foz do Iguaçu, PR: *EDITARES/CEAEC;* 8th Ed. Electronic; 2013; p. 7,943 to 7,946).

Voluntariology. A consciousness' will to do volunteer work is considered one of the most intelligent and advanced strategies in the scope of returnology. Dedication to interassistantial tasks without financial return indicates the level of lucidity already attained by the individual. Throughout decades, conscientiology has been developing its own structure, and physical and ideational sustainability as a neoscience, based on the self-empowered work of thousands of volunteers, in many different countries.

Institution. The 25 research and education institutions that make up the *International Cosmoethical Conscientiological Community* (ICCC) (base date: February 2017), each have a faculty, scientific team, and management council composed of volunteers. *He who gives first receives first.*

Authorology. Writing helpful and clarifying books on the complex realities of consciential evolution is yet another very intelligent way of exercising the *reception-donation binomial.*

Legacy. It is almost impossible to try and imagine humanity without the legacy of books written by the millions of consciousnesses who left their innovative ideas and knowledge throughout History and up to today. Probably we would not even exist as a planetary civilization without the books of the Greek philosophers, the Roman thinkers, the scribes from the Middle Ages, the ideologues of the Enlightenment, historians, scientists, free-thinkers, and novelists from all cultures and epochs.

Relevance. For Vieira (2014), the human brain and the book constitute the most relevant objects in the intraphysical dimension, both being repositories of human cognition (See **Vieira**, Waldo; *Dicionário de Argumentos da Conscienciologia* (**Dictionary of Conscientiology Arguments**); Foz do Iguaçu, PR: *EDITARES;* 2014; p. 206).

Compensation. The authors of conscientiological books fully donate the copyrights of their work to the publishers, which in turn reinvest in the publishing of new titles, thus repaying the authorial contributions received. The first example came from the proposer of the new science conscientiology who donated every copyright of his vast personal body of work. This author is also included in this privileged group of volunteer authors.

Self-responsibility. The first response of a lucid consciousness regarding having previously assumed specific evolutionary tasks is to seek to fulfil the clauses of their own existential program. Being aware of the "package" received in each new physical existence, the individual seeks to fulfil the items contained in their personal plan of interassistantial tasks, to the maximum. Those who take themselves seriously do not waste existential contributions.

To COMPENSATE FOR **CONTRIBUTIONS RECEIVED THROUGH** CLARIFYING TASKS**, FOR EXAMPLE, TEACHING, WRITING USEFUL BOOKS, AND VOLUNTEERING IS GOOD EVIDENCE OF ONE´S PERCENTAGE OF** EVOLUTIONARY INTELLIGENCE**.**

Self-questioning. How do you, reader, fare regarding the repaying of material and consciential contributions received in your present lifetime? Are you defaulting, or up to date with your evolutionary debts?

5. SENSE OF EVOLUTIONARY UTILITY

> **Useful.** In complex modern life, with variegated
> and ubiquitous causes and effects, knowing
> how to distinguish the **useful** from the *worthless*
> is the first demonstration of wisdom.[10]

Definition. The *sense of evolutionary utility* is the intimate conscential condition of self-certitude regarding having a useful existential task to be performed, for the benefit of humanity, propelling the consciousness to assistantial productivity (**Manfroi,** Eliana; *Senso de Utilidade Evolutiva* (**Sense of Evolutionary Utility**); *verbet*; In: **Vieira,** Waldo; Org.; *Encyclopaedia of Conscientiology;* defended at the *CEAEC Tertuliarium,* Foz do Iguaçu, PR, on: 20.07.2014).

Synonyms: 1. Sense of evolutionary usefulness. 2. Sense of evolutionary value. 3. Consciousness in the service of evolution. 4. Discernment of evolutionary efficacy.

Antonyms: 1. Feeling of existential void. 2. Existential unproductive consciousness. 3. Sense of antievolutionary barrenness. 4. Sense of impropriety.

---

10 **Vieira,** Waldo; *Léxico de Ortopensatas* (**Lexicon of Orthopensatas**); Foz do Iguaçu, PR: *EDITARES;* 2014; p. 1.671.

Responsibility. The sense of evolutionary utility implies self-responsibility and self-usefulness before interassistantial demands and priority evolutionary needs.

Intraconscientiality. The intimate certainty of having something important to do in one's current existence has been mentioned in the reflections of countless thinkers throughout history. This certainty may have been the driving force behind great discoveries, inventions, works and achievements of individuals who had an intimate sense of not being reborn just for "tourism".

Sense. In conscientiology this self-conviction is studied in depth and is known as the *sense of a proexis,* mainly aggregating self-awareness around the intermissivist's interassistantial and proevolutionary planning for the current human life.

Colloquiology. Who has never heard or said: *How can I help you?* Although common, this expression does not represent the real availability of many consciousnesses to selflessly serve others.

Will. The sense of evolutionary usefulness is the basis of volunteer work, as discussed in the previous chapter, where a consciousness seeks to be useful based on the donation of their own abilities or potentials to the target-public, in whatever way necessary.

Differential. Distinguishing the sense of evolutionary usefulness from *existential anxiety* becomes fundamental in the moment that a consciousness defines their megafocus, directs own choices, and makes prioritary decisions.

Angstology. *Existential angst* is the affective state of restlessness, unrest, upheaval, constant tension, and a sense of urgency usually characterized by the self-perception of an individual being late, in default, in debt, retrograde, and/or accommodated in relation to their personal and group existential program. However, some level of positive, beneficial stress is necessary for a consciousness to avoid remaining "neutral" regarding evolution.

Dispersion. It is likely that the central grievance of this pattern of antievolutionary anxiety lies in the risk of dispersion of personal efforts and energy. The urgency to accomplish something one considers important can lead a consciousness to assume too many fronts of work, because, in the logic of existential anxiety, among the dozens of tasks assumed the fundamental clause of one's life project may exist, bringing pseudorelief to the persistent internal demand.

Clause. An essential item, unmissable in the existential program, the fundamental clause determines the fulfilment of a particular act or specific incumbency indispensable in intraphysical life, required for the proexist, and chosen by themselves during the preresomatic intermissive period" (See **Vieira,** Waldo; Org.; *Cláusula Pétrea* (**Fundamental Clause**); *Encyclopaedia of Conscientiology;* Foz do Iguaçu, PR: *EDITARES/CEAEC;* 8th Ed. Electronic; 2013; p. 2,801 to 2,804).

Haste. A kind of inner calling, a sense of evolutionary usefulness, if unidentified by the consciousness, may trigger the condition of dispersion and a lack of focus on the essential, notably in this *Age of Abundance.* Accepting all the invitations and making yourself available to many different fronts of work is, probably, the way to haste and incompletism. Anxiety is quieted by a false sense of "doing a lot", but perhaps not what is essential.

THE SENSE OF EVOLUTIONARY USEFULNESS IS THE INTIMATE CERTAINTY A CONSCIOUSNESS HAS SOMETHING PRIORITARY TO ACCOMPLISH IN THEIR CURRENT HUMAN LIFE, NOTABLY AS REGARDS RECYCLING AND INTERASSISTANCE.

Self-questioning. Do you, reader, have intimate certainty of having something useful to accomplish in your current life? In which area? Do you consider yourself already fulfilling the fundamental clause of your own evolutionary task?

6. EXISTENTIAL SELF-AUDIT AND THE *AMBITIONLESSNESS TECHNIQUE*

Inventoriology. He who keeps an inventory does not need to invent fads. He knows what he needs.[11]

Definition. *Existential self-audit* is the procedure, method, or technique used by a lucid intermissivist consciousness to take inventory, examine, scan, brush up, and evaluate their own performance in the procurement of their proexes and the production of evolutionary assets, taken at any stage of their life cycle (V. **Manfroi,** Eliana; *Quinquagenarian Self-audit; verbet*; In: **Vieira,** Waldo; Org.; ***Encyclopaedia of Conscientiology;*** Foz do Iguaçu, PR: *EDITARES/CEAEC;* 8th Ed. Electronic; 2013; p. 1,235 to 1,240).

Synonyms: 1. Life self-inventory. 2. Existential accounts. 3. Self-audit to resoma. 4. Existential self-check.

Antonyms: 1. Institutional audit. 2. Existential heteroinventory.

Self-diagnosis. The self-inventory technique is something one can perform at different stages of life. The author of this book performed this self-examination at the age of 50, considering different parameters,

---

11 **Vieira,** Waldo; ***Léxico de Ortopensatas*** (**Lexicon of Orthopensatas**); Foz do Iguaçu, PR: *EDITARES;* 2014; p. 922.

such as the 25 listed below, which may also be applied and reflected upon by the reader. As a suggestion, you can evaluate the statements presented here in alphabetic order by using (1 – very little; 2 – little; 3 – more or less; 4 – a lot; 5 – very much):

01. Anticonflictology. I have a healthy self-esteem and a reasonable percentage of anticonflict in relation to my performance of my existential program.

02. Careology. I have adopted a *culture of care* in my interrelationships.

03. Codology. I have already produced and apply personal codes of conduct compatible with my current evolutionary level.

04. Contributiology. I already repay the evolutionary contributions and opportunities received.

05. Conviviology. I respect the consciential singularity and intelligence of my evolutionary co-passengers.

06. Equilibriology. I invest in useful parapsychism in the same proportion as I do my intellectuality and personal communicability.

07. Gesconology. I produce as many clarifying consciential gestations (such as books) as the number of self-overcomings I manage to do.

08. Heterocriticology. I practice constructive and cosmoethical heterocriticism most of the time.

09. Interassistantiology. I have been welcoming, empathetic, and guiding towards consciousnesses in need of assistance.

10. Liberology. I have the liberty to choose and an elevated percentage of free will.

11. Leaderology. I assume leadership roles, without pusillanimity, in face of my proexis' demands.

12. Neophilia. I have a neophilic profile, one open to new experiences in this resoma.

13. Parapedagogy. I assume a posture of semperlearner, without boasting.

14. Polyvalenciology. I face personal polyvalence and already possess an assumed interassistantial identity.

15. Psychosomatology. I cultivate interconsciential relationships of affective proximity, including with my evolutionary (affective-sexual) partner in an evolutionary duo.

16. Self-confidentology. I walk through life with self-confidence so far.

17. Self-decidology. My critical decisions are guided by my intraconsciential compass, and not just by the opinions of others.

18. Self-determinology. I have sufficient self-determination to take evolutionary choices to their ultimate cosmoethical consequences.

19. Self-evolutiology. I am relatively pleased with the balance of my self-actualizations in my current existence.

20. Self-organizatiology. I am able to successfully manage the various responsibilities assumed in my current existence.

21. Self-politicology. I have self-clarity regarding my chosen evolutionary personal political policies, and their results.

22. Self-prioriology. I have built a sufficient financial reserve to prioritize my group and personal proexis.

23. Self-recinology. I face the intraconsciential recyclings necessary to my self-evolution with fearlessness and vigour.

24. Self-relayology. If I die tomorrow, I am sure that I will leave a significant and contributory personal legacy to my evolutionary group.

25. Self-strongtraitology. I identify and apply my strongtraits (talents and skills).

Self-priorities. The self-diagnosis made by the author of this antiwastage handbook, based on her own existential self-audit, was that she was wasting contributions and opportunities, even if there was an underlying misleading sense of being aligned with her existential program, and producing "a lot". Redefining evolutionary self-priorities and making necessary adjustments were essential to bringing her life project *back on track*.

Ambitionlessness. Based on the results of her personal audit, perhaps the main technique used by the author to *correct her trajectory*, considering her existential program, was conscious detachment from certain bonds, which although positive and productive, were not yet convergent with the megafocus of the evolutionary commitments assumed. This stance was dubbed of career ambitionlessness, as in the case of the author it referred to her professional career.

Definology. *Career ambitionlessness* is the quality or state of detachment, abnegation, denial, and renunciation of a lucid consciousness in relation to their own successful professional career, still in force, through the priorities and demands of one´s personal and group existential program (V. **Manfroi,** Eliana; *verbet*; In: **Vieira,** Waldo Org.; ***Desambição Carreirística*** (Career Ambitionlessness); ***Encyclopaedia of Conscientiology;*** Foz do Iguaçu, PR: *EDITARES/CEAEC;* 8th Ed. Electronic; 2013; p. 3,884 to 3,888).

Synonymology: 1. Professional detachment. 2. Proexical prioritization. 3. Labor resignation. 4. Career detachment. 5. Cosmoethical disengagement from one´s profession.

Antonymology: 1. Career attachment. 2. Prioritization of one's profession. 3. Career-oriented.

Success. The idea of *evolutionary success* is far vaster than the concept of *professional success.* To give up your *dream work* may mean, in some cases, choosing the career of professional proevolutionary assistance. Far from signifying a vow of poverty and an "alternative" life, rather it can signify maximum prioritization and self-organization so that at a mature age one has the freedom to invest one's time, money, and energies in the success of one's proexis, with existential completism.

Complexis. *Existential completism* is the comfortable condition of completeness in relation to the satisfactory realization of a consciousness' proexis, planned in advance during the intermissive period (See **Vieira;** Waldo; *Manual da Proéxis* (**Existential Program Manual**); Rio de Janeiro, RJ: *IIPC;* 1998; p. 116).

Handcuffs. The popular expression "golden handcuffs" denotes the condition of being well-paid, but they still imprison the consciousness to a profession to the detriment of other more essential evolutionary investments (**Eliachar,** Karina; *Algema de Ouro* (**Golden handcuffs**); *verbet;* In: **Vieira,** Waldo; Org.; *Encyclopaedia of Conscientiology;* defended at the *CEAEC Tertuliarium,* Foz do Iguaçu, PR, on: 07.07.2014).

Example. The case of a *Microsoft* executive in the USA, John Wood (1930–2011), is recognized worldwide. He left his career in the stellar technology corporation, breaking his "handcuffs", and became the founder of the non-profit organization *Room to Read* (2000), which is currently active in Nepal, Vietnam, Cambodia, India, Sri-Lanka, Laos, and South Africa, imbued with the dissemination of libraries and schools.

Autobiography. The autobiographical book *Leaving Microsoft to Change the World* tells the story of his disengagement from a conventional career, but also shows his full motivation to contribute to Humanity's essential demand: education (See **Wood,** John; **Saí da Microsoft para Mudar o Mundo (Leaving Microsoft to Change the World)**; Rio de Janeiro, RJ: *Sextante;* 2007; p. 63).

Conviviology. Not always is one's choice well understood. For example, here are 6 typical reactions from co-workers, bosses, friends, and family members regarding a professionally ambitionless consciousness, and their definitive move out of a successful career. The examples are listed in a probable order of occurrence:

1. **Amazement:** *"X resigned!"; "That can't be true!"*

2. **Disdain:** *"She's left, she was going to be let go anyways..."; "She became a fanatic!"; "She's lost her mind!"*

3. **Commiseration:** *"Poor thing, she's going to regret it!"; "She's made the biggest mistake of her life"*

4. **Envy:** *"Lucky one!"; "I wish I could do the same!"; "One of these days I'm going to get there!"*

5. **Admiration:** *"Brave girl!"; "A living lesson to her colleagues!"*

6. **Understanding:** *"She's going to be a volunteer"; "She has another life project".*

Characterology. The profile of a career-detached consciousness may show, for example, 10 intraconsciential characteristics, facilitating and/or propelling their career ambitionlessness. It is worth a reader interested using the technique to check their own ambitionlessness profile:

01. **Decidophilia** (firmness in decisions).

02. **Evolutionary assertiveness.**

03. **Financial intelligence.**

04. **Healthy self-esteem.**

05. **Intelligent fearlessness.**

06. **Interassistantial self-motivation.**

07. **Proexological megafocus.**

08. **Self-confidence.**

09. **Self-organization.**

10. **Volitiophilia** (ironclad resolve).

Proexis. It should be emphasized the fact that not every profession necessarily constitutes a personal proexis. However, there are situations in which a professional activity can function as a bridge or support to one's existential project. The lucidity to make such a distinction is developed through deep self-research and assumption of the role of a minicog within the evolutionary maximechanism.

Lucidity. To apply the *career ambitionlessness technique* requires lucidity, self-organization, and maturity from those who adopt it. To give up on something that society values and encourages is not an easy decision, and all the consequences should be considered and pondered. Self-determination and the intimate sense of the prioritary evolutionary career are at the base of the aplication of this technique.

Indication. It is not the objective of this book to unrestrictedly prescribe this strategy, nor is it the author's focus for being a non-career driven person. However, identification of those close to her who also took this option and the resulting interassistantial results affirm the correctness of the choice. Nevertheless, such an option is not yet feasible for all intermissivists, but it may already be the lucid option for many.

*B*REAKING ONE'S "*GOLDEN HANDCUFFS*" DENOTES A CONSIDERABLE PERCENTAGE OF *EVOLUTIONARY INTELLIGENCE* **MANIFESTED** BY A **SELF-EFFACING** CONSCIN IN THEIR PROFESSION, YET AMBITIOUS CONCERNING THE *EVOLUTIONARY CAREER*.

Self-questioning. Have you, reader, already done a self-audit of your own life, regardless of your age? What were the results? Do you think that, together with your personal career, there may be a call for becoming a professional in assistance, via cosmoethical volunteering?

7. HYPERCRITICAL LIFE

Self-determination. The **waste of evolutionary opportunities** in consecutive human lives, after identifying one's own critical retrolife shows the consciousness' lack of self-determination.[12]

Definition. A *critical life* is a resoma, the intraphysical existence of a consciousness, in which there were significant successes or fewer mistakes and omissions, with repercussions for a large number of individuals, and influencing the successive lives of all involved.

Synonyms: 1. Critical existence. 2. Decisive life. 3. Turning point resoma.

Antonyms: 1. Common life. 2. Mediocre existence. 3. Incipient resoma.

Premise. Waldo Vieira's assertion that our current life has the value of 15 prior ones is an indicator of the relevance of our current megacritical existence.

Evolution. The critical life of a consciousness influences its *Personal Evolutionary File* (PEF), the individualized *dossier* showing the

---

12 **Vieira,** Waldo; Vieira. ***Léxico de Ortopensatas*** (**Lexicon of Orthopensatas**); Foz do Iguaçu, PR: *EDITARES;* 2014; p. 188.

balance of your evolutionary correctness throughout your human lives. The quality of this *self-evolutionary portfolio* may well have been fundamental to grant you access to the first *Intermissive Course* registered on this planet. It is probable that a critical assistantial past life was the passport for a current intermissivist preresomatic course (See **Vieira,** Waldo; ***Léxico de Ortopensatas*** **(Lexicon of Orthopensatas)**; Foz do Iguaçu, PR: *Editares International Association;* 2014; p. 1.471 and 1.472)

Relevance. Knowing critical retrolives seems to be of relevance only if it is to enrich the present existence, such as for the identification of an idle proevolutionary ability awaiting lucid and useful application. Notwithstanding, our current existence is not just critical – it is *hypercritical.*

Definition. A *hypercritical life* is the intermissivist's current existence, in the 21st century, with an abundance of existential inputs and opportunities available, in a scale never seen before throughout the evolutionary trajectory of this orb (See **Vieira,** Waldo; ***Léxico de Ortopensatas*** **(Lexicon of Orthopensatas)**; Foz do Iguaçu, PR: *Editares International Association;* 2014; p. 1,063, 1,068 and 1,575).

Synonyms: 1. Present hypercritical existence. 2. Resoma of evolutionary megaimpact.

Antonyms: 1. Hypermediocre life. 2. *Lukewarm* evolutionary existence.

Affinities. Personal interests and affinities in our present-day human life are signs of a critical retrolife of a consciousness. Such a past life may be the root of one´s current innate ideas and personal success, as well as of present intolerances and aversions. The person´s "way", their temperament, mirror prior existences due to the fact that we have the same set of memories (holomemory), abilities, and also immaturities to be overcome (See **Fernandes**, Pedro; ***Retrovida Crítica*** (**Critical Retrolife**); *verbet*; In: **Vieira,** Waldo; Org.; ***Encyclopaedia of Conscientiology;*** defended at the *CEAEC Tertuliarium,* Foz do Iguaçu, PR, on: 18.06.2016).

Omission. Just as important as what the consciousness achieved during an evolutionary favourable critical existence, is that of what it did not achieve, that what they could have done and *left undone.* This is a deficit omission. The consciousness could have done even better.

Paradox. On the other hand, the concept of *surplus omission* (omisur) advocates the fact that, in a given existence, due to the *zeitgeist,* prevailing values, and personal evolutionary level, the consciousness could have committed more mistakes and follies, but *didn't.* The consciousness could have done worse, but didn't make those mistakes.

Cleavage. The experience of critical situations may trigger a process of evolutionary cleavage, which is the experience the intra or extraphysical consciousness has of a *de facto* forceful, incisive self-decision, that promoted a cleft, splitting, and differentiation in their own existential *continuum,* as in the *before* and *after* of that particular critical evolutionary experience. (See **Manfroi,** Eliana; ***Clivagem Evolutiva* Evolutionary Cleavage**); *verbet;* In: **Vieira,** Waldo; Org.; ***Encyclopaedia of Conscientiology;*** defended at the *CEAEC Tertuliarium,* Foz do Iguaçu, PR, on: 04.09.2013).

Example. As examples, here are, listed in alphabetic order, 8 possible experiences of the consciousness, capable of promoting an evolutionary cleavage with different existential consequences:

1. **Decision.** Magnum self-decisions aligning the axis of the proexis.

2. **Encounter.** *Encounters with fate* that change evolutionary routes.

3. **Habits.** A radical, compulsory change of personal habits and routines.

4. **Maxidissidence.** Leaving a group that restricts one's freedom of expression.

5. **Moratory.** Survival of a near-fatal accident.

6. **Neoperspective.** The reperspectivation of one's existence before neoideas.

7. **Recycling.** Serious somatic disease generating self-recycling.

8. **Values.** An axiological shock renovating personal values.

Abundance. It is worth the reader reflecting on, specifically, 8 compelling arguments, selected by this author, which support the hypothesis of our current **hypercritical life**, presented by Vieira (See **Vieira**, Waldo; *Dicionário de Argumentos da Conscienciologia* (**Dictionary of Conscientiology Arguments**); Foz do Iguaçu, PR: *EDITARES;* 2014; p. 163, 208, 464, 756, 819, 877 and 1,002):

1. *"We have never enjoyed in our past human lives on this planet such an abundance of readings, approaches, and research as in this 21st century. It is time to take advantage of the mentalsomatic resources, with criteria, and self and heterocriticism."*

2. *"We have never enjoyed, in our past human lives over the millennia, so many factors simultaneously converging to the increment of consciential evolution. Self-experience and self-organization have never been so relevant as now, in the 21st century. Therein lies the megafocus-megapriority binomial."*

3. *"At no time, as now, have we faced so many challenges of consciential expansion through the evolutionary priorities evident, unmissable,*

and at hand. *Self-effort and self-reflection are hence worth it. The facts and parafacts are here for you to see, irreducible. It's time to stop pussyfooting around."*

4. *"Intraphysical life has never required so much analysis of contents of evolutionary priorities as it has today, in the 21st century, due to the technological complexities of modern life."*

5. *"Thus, the new science conscientiology, based on the new paradigm of consciousness, itself, and on consciential energies (CEs) – the two basic realities or pararealities in the cosmos, compose a corpus of neoverpons unlike anything before in the history of mankind, far beyond sciences, philosophies, religions, politics, sports, arts and crafts that have been governing people, races, and nations over the millennia."*

6. *"Due to the extraphysical reurbanization (reurbex) of planet earth, and its consequent intraphysical reurbanization (reurbin), terrestrial recycling, or this human dimension, the present interdimensional interchange in humanity, although not so visible, is the most intense throughout History (Age of Acceleration of Human History)."*

7. *"At 03:15 of a silent dawn, I felt the presence of the serenissimus codenamed "Monja" (Nun), who telepathized: – In all of Human History, no consciousness, including those you call serenissimi, even left the legacy of a corpus of knowledge such as that of conscientiology to Humanity. See your personal responsibilities in the context of such a venture with your volunteers."*

8. *"In this 21st century, and third millennium, we live in the Age of Abundance. Thus, the most intelligent and consistent with the zeitgeist is to*

act with the mentalsoma to the maximum of our possibilities and creativity, expanding our orthothosenes,[13] including those heterocritical."

OUR CURRENT HYPERCRITICAL LIFE **DEMANDS MAXIMUM EVALUATION AND PLANNING. MISTAKES AND OMISSIONS,** IN OUR CONDITION WEIGH **15** TIMES MORE. **THE SAME** IS **VALID FOR** SUCCESSES AND SELF-OVERCOMINGS.

Questionings. Have you, the reader, already assessed the importance of the *evolutionary capitalization* of your current resoma? Have you considered, in *existential economic* terms, the high profitability of your current cosmoethical correctness?

---

13 Orthothosene is the consciousness' cosmoethical and fraternal *tho*ught+*sen*timent+energy (thosene).

SECTION II
WASTOLOGY

8. An Age of Wastage

> **Self-discernment.** We cannot take advantage
> of everything in life; however, it is not good
> to maintain idle capacities. If a person is
> polyvalent, they end up wasting something,
> but it is not wise to waste what is **essential.**[14]

Wastage. *Wastage* is the act or effect of wasting, overspending, or squandering evolutionary values with neither discretion nor profit (See **Vieira,** Waldo; Org.; ***Desperdício* (Wastage);** *Encyclopaedia of Conscientiology;* Foz do Iguaçu, PR: *EDITARES/CEAEC;* 2013; p. 3,977 to 3,980).

Definition. *Age of Wastage* is the historical epoch or time period hypothetically starting at the end of the 20th century, characterized by squandering, or waste of all kinds of resources and subsidies available to human population.

Synonyms: 1. *Age of Spending.* 2. *Age of Lavishness.* 3. *Age of Recklessness.* 4. Cycle of Wastage.

Antonyms: 1. *Age of Abundance.* 2. *The Heyday.* 3. *Age of Recycling. 4. Cycle of Reuse.*

Paradox. It is paradoxical to realize that our current *Age of Abundance* coexists with the *Age of Wastage.* Civilizations produce vast amounts

---

14 **Vieira,** Waldo; ***Léxico de Ortopensatas* (Lexicon of Orthopensatas);** Foz do Iguaçu, PR: *EDITARES;* 2014; p. 192.

of consumer goods, but at the same time squander said production without rational criteria.

Planet. Since the beginning of the 21st century, environmental scientists, economists, sociologists, and global thinkers have reiterated that we are consuming planetary reserves of resources necessary for human survival (and also for the survival of all other species). Mankind is self-serving, dishing up as if at a *planetary banquet table* until there is nothing left to consume. With such wastage of the supposedly never-ending abundant natural resources, one may die of starvation in the near future (See **Oliveira,** Gesner; ***O Fim da Era do Desperdício* (The end of the Age of Wastage);** *Veja;* São Paulo, SP: *Editora Abril,* 06.08.2014; p. 17 to 21).

Footprint. The Swiss Mathis Wackernagel (1962–), whose doctoral thesis brought the concept of *ecological footprint,* warns us of the fact that Humanity is going deep into a *planetary overdraft,* spending 20% more than the renewal capacity of the resources. For Wackernagel, we need to either reduce expenditure (consumption) or increase revenue (planet). It is evident that we cannot expand Earth, except by colonizing other planets. The solution is to cut superfluous expenses and wastage of all kinds.

Tool. The ecological footprint proposes a tool that calculates the quantity of natural resources consumed compared to resources available. About 4 centuries ago, British economist Thomas Malthus (1766–1834) already warned about population growth in the future surpassing the capacity to feed so many mouths. By 2050, according to the UN, there will be more than 10 billion mouths to feed. Surveys show that half the food produced on the planet is wasted.

Modernity. Polish sociologist Zygmunt Bauman (1925–2017) is the proposer of the approach to *Liquid Modernity* (2001) and the current *Liquid Life* (2009) (the titles of 2 of his many books). The metaphor relates the *fluidity* of Society in late 20th and early 21st century, marked by the instability of institutions, values, and principles of the postmodern world (See **Zygmunt,** Bauman; ***Modernidade Líquida*** **(Liquid Modernity)**; Rio de Janeiro, RJ: *Zahar;* 2001; p. 7 to 12).

Consumption. Bauman argues that the current condition of excess of possibilities and choice generates anxiety and anguish, due to the impermanence of everything – from objects to human relationships. An example of this fluidity is hyperconsumerism and the permanent discarding of things so a new acquisition can take place, in an endless cycle of consumption, garbage generation, and waste of planetary resources.

Garbage. To this sociologist, the garbage produced on a gigantic scale constitutes the most abundant product of our *liquid-modern society of consumption.* Garbage is not only solid waste, like your old refrigerator that has become *obsolete,* but also when relationships, values, and patterns of behaviour become voraciously consumed and discarded.

Self-obsolescence. To become obsolete or be discarded is the fear of this liquid modernity, leading individuals to compulsively seek out the latest and most *fashionable clothes, haircut, car of the year,* and above all *the newest trendiest pattern of behaviour*, which will make a "visible and differentiated" person within the multitude of *equal* beings.

Validity. The *Age of Wastage* can be characterized by the *best before date culture:* ready-to consume, easily discarded, as tomorrow there will be something better to buy. Products, behaviours, and lifestyles all have an increasingly shorter *expiry date.*

Desire. The root of this vicious cycle lies in the *culture of hedonism* of the present *Age of Lavishness.* It is the immediate satisfaction of desires, impulses, and whims, without reflection on the evolutionary worth of all this consumption.

Excess. Bauman synthesizes the current confusion of values and behaviours of liquid modernity in the expression: *excess no longer seems excessive, nor does waste seem a loss.* It is hedonistic voracity.

Effects. Excess (abundance) and wastage, when placed side by side in interaction, can generate a disastrous connection. However, the evolutionary effects can be even more devastating when they refer to self-waste.

Definition. The *interaction: abundance-wastage* is the mutual influence or reciprocal action of the conditions of material and informational abundance, as well as of evolutionary opportunities offered by contemporaneity, and the response to deprioritization, neglect, trivialization, and waste of reckless conscins, members of the pathological intraphysical society (See **Manfroi**, Eliana; *Interação Farturologia-Desperdiciologia* (**Abundanceology-Wastology Interaction**); *verbet*; In: **Vieira**, Waldo; Org.; *Encyclopaedia of Conscientiology;* defended at the *CEAEC Tertuliarium,* Foz do Iguaçu, PR, on: 13.12.2013).

Synonyms: 1. *Interaction generosity-prodigality.* 2. *Interaction Age of Abundance–Age of Wastage.* 3. Opulence-squandering binomial.

Antonyms: 1. *Advantage-contribution interaction.* 2. *Interaction scarcity-waste.* 3. Antagonism Deficienciology / Abundanceology.

Megadiscard. Considering the increasing technological avalanche, humanity has been faced with the challenge of the *hyperconsumerism-megadiscard binomial.* It is common to find in mobile phone shops, for example, the possibility of discarding devices probably initially bought in the very same shop. Paradox: the same place that sells a supposedly durable device already provides a place to discard it, in the near future.

Abundanceland. It is *Abundanceland* transformed into a *Wasteland.*

Bankruptcy. Generally, one records large expenditures, but it is the sum of the small wastages that drive a company or an existential program to bankruptcy.

Typology. In the midst of all this, consciential wastage is the most harmful type of squander. In the next chapter we will discuss 4 types of squandering, with obvious antievolutionary effects: time, money, talents, and self-reflection.

THE INTERACTION ABUNDANCE-WASTAGE CLARIFIES THE CURRENT MOMENT OF SOCIETY, BOUND BY ANTIDISCERNMENT BEFORE THE MEGOPPORTUNITY OF EVOLUTIONARY ACCELERATION AND PLANETARY RECYCLING.

Self-questioning. Do you, reader, identify hyperconsumerism in your behaviour?

9. Typology of Antievolutionary Wastes

> **Time.** Time is yours to use. Each day has
> 1,440 minutes. Each minute is unique. –
> "How do you spend this treasure?" [15]

Relevance. Relating all kinds of contemporary wastes would require a book on its own. In the author's view, the choice of the 4 types developed in this chapter respects the relevance of these aspects to our current hypercritical life. **Time and money,** the first two presented, although somewhat intraphysical, may lead to losing an existential program, if poorly administered. The next two, **talents and self-reflection,** are of an intraconsciential nature and essential resources to complete one's evolutionary life project, as they constitute a sort of compass for the consciousness to find its personal *Evolutionary North*, the guidelines of one's existential self-programming.

WASTE OF TIME

Convention. The feeling of not having time for anything permeates the existence of many consciousnesses. Time is an intraphysical,

---

15 **Vieira,** Waldo; *Léxico de Ortopensatas* **(Lexicon of Orthopensatas);** Foz do Iguaçu, PR: *EDITARES;* 2014; p. 1,609.

human convention to help us organize the succession of events from the past, present and into the future. However, the only possible *time* of objective consciential activity is the present.

Opportunity. In dictionaries, it is possible to find one of the most enlightening meanings of the word being scrutinized: *an opportunity to accomplish something.* In relation to the proexis, it is precisely this concept that is of interest to a level-headed intermissivist.

Fear. Fear of performing a task can consume more time and energy than actually doing it. What is the consciential trait at the root of intraconsciential and intraphysical time-wasting? Self-disorganization? Lack of prioritization? Lack of focus? Fear of success and responsibility that such a situation may entail?

Procrastination. Procrastinating, or dallying away, may cover a fear of criticism and/or self-excuse in the argument that a particular task was lacking, it was not as well done as it could have been, because "it was done at the last minute".

Excuse. The self-deceptive idea of working better under pressure is one of the mottos of time saboteurs. Meeting deadlines at the last minute may indicate an addiction to adrenaline.

Tasks. Another waste of time and energy is to interrupt a task (that you could have continued to completion) and then have to restart the work. To finish what one has begun, whenever possible, is self-deintruding as it frees one´s self-thosenity and mind to new challenges, leaving us intraconscientially space for new ideas.

Efficiency. Retrieving necessary information that is disorganized, can represent a drain of available time that otherwise could have been applied to one's productivity. Hence the importance of self-organization to immediately find the records, materials, and documents required.

Have you, reader, already lost hours looking for a file or document that *you were sure you had left there, somewhere,* in the mountain of paper in front of you?

Benefits. The benefits of organization can only be understood by a self-organized conscin, when they obtain maximum productivity in the application of their own time.

Techniques. It is relatively easy to find in bookshops dozens of books with techniques to escape *the time trap.* What is difficult is to acquire and maintain new habits and proficient routines.

Discernment. Nevertheless, the most advanced technologies will prove innocuous when seeking to solve the absence of the basic attribute in *chronocides*: discernment regarding the importance of the good evolutionary use of time, in full force, during the hypercritical current human life (See **Mackenzie,** Alec; ***A Armadilha do Tempo: Como Implantar Plano de Ação Individual e Coletivo para o Melhor Aproveitamento do Tempo*** (**The Time Trap**); São Paulo, SP: *Makron, Mcgraw Books;* 1991; p. 228 to 245).

Behaviour. If, hypothetically, a researcher were to accompany you, the reader, throughout an entire week, observing all your activities, and without knowing your intentions, what could this researcher tell about your priorities from this observation of your use of time?

Resource. Time is an existential resource, and the way in which a consciousness invests this "asset" leaves clues about the consciousness' values and of what really matters to them. The way in which a person uses their time is a strong indicator of what is really the priority in their existence.

Waste. A researcher of the human habit of procrastination, Piers Steel (1967–), notes in his book *The Procrastination Equation: How to Stop Putting Things Off and Start Getting Stuff Done* (2012), that the hours wasted without the slightest concern are becoming increasingly more limited and precious. Wasted hours, according to this author, when summed, can give you the sensation that you are wasting your life. Unfortunately, this is not just a sensation; it is a fact (See **Steel,** Piers. *A Equação de Deixar para Depois (The Procrastination Equation: How to Stop Putting Things Off and Start Getting Stuff Done);* Rio de Janeiro, RJ: *BestSeller;* 2012; p. 16 and 17).

Self-questioning. You could ask yourself: in which evolutionary priorities should I be investing my time?

WASTE OF MONEY

Value. Like time, money is a quantifying resource for personal values. Those who have a proexis and take the condition seriously do not waste financial resources.

Behaviour. Where you apply your money can say a lot about what you consider essential in your existence. The financial life of an intraphysical consciousness should be managed by rational and evolutionary criteria. However, human behaviour related to personal finances has been more controlled by the psychosoma (emotion) than the mentalsoma (rationality).

Proexis. *Proexogenic financial intelligence* is the capacity of the conscin to apply their cognitive functions, discernment, and the ability to deal with finances, envisaging the acquisition, conservation, and multiplication of their financial resources with the aim of attaining their personal and group existential program (proexis) (See **Leite,** Hernande; *Inteligência Financeira Proexogênica* (**Proexogenice Financial Intelligence**); *verbet;* In: **Vieira,** Waldo; Org.; *Encyclopaedia of Conscientiology;* Foz do Iguaçu, PR: *EDITARES/CEAEC;* 8th Ed. Electronic; 2013; p. 6,114 to 6,123).

Patrimony. Developing this kind of intelligence is fundamental for antiwasting intermissivists. Investing in personal and group self-evolution is the best possible destination available to your money which, like time, is a means to evolution, and not its purpose.

Drain. Consumerist psychosomatic behaviour is characterized by the acquisition of goods without discernment. Buying on impulse and not delaying desires and satisfaction will not only affect your budget but above all *pull the rug from under your feet.*

Test. Here is a challenge for the reader who may wish to ask themselves the following 12 questions about their consumption habits, and take their own conclusions:

01. Do you buy more clothes than you can use?

02. Do you buy household items that stay stored in the closet?

03. Do you visit *shopping centres* and spend when you feel lonely, bored or sad?

04. Do you give presents to people outside of commemorative dates just to please them, or out of guilt?

05. Do you redecorate your home every 12 months just to "refresh" the environment?

06. Do you get *loans* to pay for *loans*?

07. Do you lose control of your credit card, paying only the minimum amount?

08. Have you not been able to save something at the end of the month for over a year?

09. Do you prefer to change car instead of having health insurance or a health plan?

10. Do you sometimes buy useless stuff due to not being able to resist sales?

11. Do you plan your purchases? Do you take a list with you to the supermarket?

12. Do you throw away food because the products have passed their expiry date?

Self-investment. Applying financial resources to self-qualification and interassistance shows a reasonable percentage of *evolutionary intelligence*. Here are, as examples, 8 suggestions for proexogenic investments listed in alphabetical order:

1. **Authorship.** Sponsor your own clarifying book, also donating the copyright.

2. **Books.** Acquire books and other artefacts of knowledge to expand your personal erudition.

3. **Entrepreneurship.** Promote cosmoethical patronage, financing evolutionary enterprises.

4. **Foresight.** Make financial provision for contingencies.

5. **Honesty.** Ensure the origin of your income, making sure you receive *clean* money.

6. **Self-organization.** Seek financial self-organization so you can give yourself and others presents, without feeling guilty.

7. **Travel.** Invest, if possible, in travel for self and heteroresearch.

8. **Volunteering.** Finance your own voluntary work in a proevolutionary institution.

Self-questioning. Is there better return for the useful application of a consciousness' financial wealth than an investing in their own evolution?

WASTE OF TALENTS

Setbacks. Adversity can play a paradoxical role in one´s existence. Setbacks, in some cases, are opportunities to recover dormant talents.

Self-waste. Possessing specific abilities, skills, and intelligences and not applying such personal resources, neither in your own favour, nor in favour of others, characterizes a grossly *ignorant consciousness*. To waste strongtraits, one´s evolutionary talents, is one of the greatest squanders in this *Age of Abundance*.

Income. Talents can be divided in 2 categories:

1. **Pointless:** burdensome, idle, and fruitless.

2. **Profitable:** lucrative, productive, and fruitful.

Idleness. An *idle or a dormant strongtrait* is a strongtrait or positive component of a consciousness' microuniverse that is kept inactive, sterile, underused, unprofitable, weakened, abandoned, latent in the intraconsciential manifestation, and neglected in the dynamization of the evolutionary recyclings of one´s self-proexis (See **Rossa**, Dayane; *Trafor Ocioso* (**Idle strongtrait**); *verbet;* In: **Vieira**, Waldo; Org.; ***Encyclopaedia of Conscientiology;*** Foz do Iguaçu, PR: *EDITARES/CEAEC;* 8th Ed. Electronic; 2013; p. 10,618 to 10,623).

Intelligence. Paraphrasing the American journalist Barbara Strauch (1951–2015), individuals of all ages have, in the 21st century, *the best brain out of all their lives*. People are becoming smarter, tachypsychic, and paradoxically many of them waste a great deal of these cognitive skills

(See **Strauch,** Barbara; ***O Melhor Cérebro da sua Vida: Segredos e Talentos da Ma-turidade*** (**The Secret Life of the Grown-up Brain: The Surprising Talents of the Middle-Aged Mind**); Rio de Janeiro, RJ: *Zahar;* 2011; p. 37 to 41).

Paradox. The paradoxical situation is that the most intelligent and talented consciousnesses may be the most wasted, due to their polyvalence and dispersiveness before so many possibilities of doing almost everything *well,* lacking the lucidity to prioritize what is evolutionarily relevant. This *blindness* can have its roots in boasting and personal pride.

Research. The psychologist Alexander Penney (PhD), of MacEwan University in Canada, has published research on the relationship between a high intelligence quotient (IQ) and anxiety. The researcher interviewed college students and discovered that those with higher IQs were the most anxious.

Good-sense. In summary, the research concluded that greater intelligence is not necessarily tantamount to having discernment to make wiser and more sensible decisions (See **Robson,** David; ***O Surpreendente Lado Ruim de Ser Inteligente*** (**The Surprising Downsides of Being Clever**); available at: http://www.bbc.com/portuguese/noticias/2015/04/150417_vert_Lado_ruim_inteligencia_ml; accessed on 14.05.16).

Trap. In general, the versatility of a polyvalent consciousness characterizes intermissivists, posing a high risk for the self-wastage of talents. Those accepted into a preresomatic qualification earned a vacancy in the *Intermissive Course* because in a previous life, or lives, they provided some kind of assistance to other consciousnesses. Cognitive skills and a diversity of experiences, many in leadership roles, accumulated in successive existences, forged the polyvalence of intermissivists (See **Vieira,** Waldo; ***Parapolimatia* (Parapolymathy);** *verbet;* In:**Vieira,** Waldo; Org.; ***Encyclopaedia of Conscientiology;*** Foz do Iguaçu, PR: *EDITARES/CEAEC;* 8th Ed. Electronic; 2013; p. 8,111 to 8,113).

Resources. Personal talents and strongtraits, when proevolutionary, are the main resources to implement one's existential program. A consciousness inherits from itself its consciential attributes and abilities developed in successive resomas.

Update. There are consciousnesses who are self-destructive, and do not use the resources of their holomemory, the repository of their personal past lives and experiences, including their strongtraits. Existential completism is to also update and qualify these abilities, offering your skills to the evolutionary market, whose current demand is for interassistance.

Megastrongtrait. Megastrongtrait is one's main talent, which when not wasted, sustains one's self-proexis, like a consciousness' *business card*. It becomes paradoxical when a person does not know and hence cannot apply their most advanced evolutionary skill, obvious to those they live among. Evolutionary geniality also consists of the fact that a consciousness distributes and constributes with its clarifying congnitive dividends.

WASTE OF SELF-REFLECTION

Excess. The abundance of technological, visual, auditory, and ideational stimuli, sometimes consumed concomitantly, compromises the consciousness' productive introspection, their self-reflection.

Immersion. Wasting opportunities for a self-reflexive immersion in themes relevant to the evolutionary moment increases the chances of making wrong decisions, or even antievolutionary inaction.

Technique. Faced with an avalanche of glitz and demands of this *Age of Abundance,* allocating time for a *self-criticism session* and personal reassessment may seem like a waste of time. Hence the novelty (in this restless contemporaneity) of the *5-hour self-reflection technique* proposed by Vieira (See **Vieira,** Waldo; Org.; ***Autorreflexão de 5 Horas* (5-Hour Self-reflection Technique);** *Encyclopaedia of Conscientiology;* Foz do Iguaçu, PR: *EDITARES/ CEAEC;* 8th Ed. Electronic; 2013; p. 2,011 to 2,014).

Prophylaxis. To dedicate 5 hours to perform a soliloquy aimed at understanding and deepening an individual's critical theme can lead to the proevolutionary referral of an existential decision capable of reverberating for the rest of one's life. One moment of insanity may require centuries of recomposition.

*WASTING TIME, MONEY, AND TALENTS **WILL DEMAND GREATER EFFORT FROM THE SELF-SQUANDERING CONSCIN,** AS DISPERSION, DISORGANIZATION, AND LACK OF SELF-REFLECTION COMPROMISE **ESSENTIAL AREAS OF** HUMAN EXISTENCE.*

Self-questioning. If you, reader, consider it difficult to evolve with your already acquired self-competences, imagine doing it in total ignorance of your own abilities?

10. Pathologies of Abundance

Excesses. Abundance leads to excess,
squandering, and extravagances.[16]

Definition. *Pathologies of abundance* constitute the set of holosomatic disorders generated by all types of excesses practiced by conscins unaware of the rational and proevolutionary use of the resources of intraphysicality.

Synonyms: 1. *Syndromes of abundance.* 2. Diseases of consumerism. 3. Nosographies of the *Age of Abundance.*

Antonyms: 1. Prophylaxis of compulsivity. 2. Avoidance of hyperconsumerism.

Pseudorelief. The main characteristic of compulsive behaviour is the absence of self-control of one's actions, and the temporary pseudorelief of anxiety and anguish (See **VandenBos,** Gary R.; Org.; ***Dicionário de Psicologia da APA** (APA Dictionary of Psychology);* Porto Alegre, RS: *Artmed;* 2010; p. 205). While the intraconsciential cause of the pattern of anxiety goes

---

16 **Vieira,** Waldo; ***Léxico de Ortopensatas** (Lexicon of Orthopensatas);* Foz do Iguaçu, PR: *EDITARES;* 2014; p. 670.

undiagnosed and not confronted, successive waves of compulsiveness alternate, generating dysfunctions in various aspects of life.

Dysfunctionality. Hyperconsumerism is an example of this dysfunctional behaviour (See **Fernandes;** Pedro; *Síndrome do Hiperconsumismo* (**Hyperconsumerism Syndrome**); *verbet;* In: **Vieira,** Waldo; Org.; *Encyclopaedia of Conscientiology;* Foz do Iguaçu, PR: *EDITARES/CEAEC;* 8th Ed. Electronic; 2013; p. 9,953 to 9,958).

Compulsion. In this *Age of Abundance* compulsive behaviours also find raw- material for feedback. Never have so many opportunities for the acquisition of assets been available to mankind, requiring even greater discernment from us.

Excess. The mass production of objects, and the constant generation of insatiable pseudoneeds, moves a voracious mechanism that consumes financial resources and generates pathologies of excess, such as compulsory accumulation, and obesity.

Commodities. Bauman synthesizes the paradox of hyperconsumerism in this sentence: – *The most prominent feature of a consumer society, even when carefully disguised and concealed – is that consumers become commodities* (See **Bauman,** Zygmunt; *Vida para Consumo: A Transformação de Pessoas em Mercadorias* (**Consuming Life, italics translated from the Portuguese**); Rio de Janeiro, RJ: *Jorge Zahar Ed.;* 2008; p. 70).

Uselessness. The connection between the *Age of Abundance* and the *Age of Wastage* generated *industries of futility* and a new type of consumption – that of all sorts of pointless things.

Dictionary. A dictionary of pointless things is a *pointlessionary.* The Portuguese neologism was proposed by Dr Waldo Vieira, and it comprehends numerous areas of human life (See **Vieira,** Waldo; *Dicionário de Argumentos da Conscienciologia* (**Dictionary of Conscientiology Arguments**); Foz do

Iguaçu, PR: *EDITARES;* 2014; p. 783). Besides objects, the Abundanceland of pointless things generates a new type of product and a new type of consumer: the emotional product and the *devourer* of emotional nonsense (See **Manfroi,** Eliana; ***Tolicionário Afetivo*** (**Emotional Nonsensionary**); *verbet;* In: **Vieira,** Waldo; Org.; ***Encyclopaedia of Conscientiology;*** defended at the *CEAEC Tertuliarium,* Foz do Iguaçu, PR, on: 13.12.2013).

Exaggeratiology. It is worth mentioning 14 areas of profitable commercial activity (Base year: 2017), characterized by their exaggerated emotional appeal, but still consumed in large scale in a list of *nonsense for sale:*

01. **Melodramatic film industry:** simplistic romantic comedies, tearjerker TV series, *pink* films for teenagers, and infantilized animated cartoons for adults.

02. **Pet-humanization industry:** birthday parties, pet *wedding* celebrations, pet carnival costumes, jewellery for animals, the canine Easter egg, and sophisticated outfits for pets.

03. **Monarchy industry:** the obsolete royal families maintaining tourism with *pomp and circumstance,* the gossip magazines delving into the royals' lives, their celebrations, royal weddings, and the birth of royal babies.

04. **Sacralization industry:** religious tourism, the sale of relics, the music of clerical-singers, cassocked celebrities, the commerce of divine favours to generous contributors, overpriced pilgrimages.

05. **Overexposure industry:** celebrity magazines, gossip TV programs, the *red carpets* of artistic awards, the *walk of fame,* the unearthed scandals.

06. **TV soap opera industry:** the Brazilian *Hollywood* of soap operas, romantic folklore themes, the caricature and shallow approaches

to social issues, popular taste for soaps, typical cultural product for exports, *fast and easily* swallowed plots and infrequent reflection.

07. **Graduation industry:** lavish ceremonies, pyrotechnic shows, fancy graduation parties, togas, gowns, speeches, and boring tributes.

08. **Wedding industry:** themed weddings, bizarre parties, nuptials at Disneyland, or at *earth's paradises* costing thousands of dollars, 24-hour open wedding chapels *(Las Vegas),* overproduced stag and hen parties, *lingerie showers,* millionaire *shows* during posh weddings, and collective Eastern weddings.

09. **Valentine industry:** matrimonial agencies, the appealing gift industry, themed dinners, hotel special packages, romantic messages on billboards, spectacular engagements, unusual requests for the *lady's* hand.

10. **Romantic tourism industry:** paradisiac itineraries for spouses, hotels with themed bridal suites, matchmaking sea cruises, excursions for singles, packages for flirty elders.

11. **Videoclip industry:** cinematographic productions, erotic appeal, songs with baratropospheric lyrics, exploitation of the gynosoma as an object, the apology of transgression, musical mediocrity.

12. **Coming of age party industry:** *"Quinceanera", "sweet fifteen"*; «*coming-out*" and "*debutante*" parties; adolescent rites of passage; mega-parties; the "live-cake"; the "*doll hand-overs*" and "*swap of ballerinas for high-heeled shoe*" rituals; debutante balls presented by celebrities; the *princess' day.*

13. **Reality show industry:** "Big Brother", the panopticon, public private lives, irrational competition, the justification of ends, inhumane physical tests, the *"anything for money" principle,* the emotional out-of-control *live.*

14. ***Pink* publishing industry:** the "literature for *little women*", tear jerking texts, emotional self-help books, romantic vampires' trilogy, *light* erotic novels for ladies.

Neopathologies. Among the neopathologies of this *Age of Abundance,* we highlight the following 3, related to the profusion of unnecessary objects, abundance of food, and excessive risky activities, presented in alphabetic order:

1. **Accumulation disorder.** The diagnosis of this disorder is recent. The psychopathology is characterized by excessive consumption and retention of objects, including garbage, without being able to discard items, to the point of cluttering entire rooms or even an entire house, preventing even the residents to enter. These are compulsive hoarders. This pathology is also known as disposophobia, or the fear of discarding objects (See **Lilienfeld,** Scott O.; **Arkowitz,** H.; *A Vida em Desordem* **(Life in Disarray)**; *Mente & Cérebro;* magazine; São Paulo, SP: Editora Segmento, 2014; p. 50 to 53).

Trash. Every useless object accumulated by a consciousness ends up transforming itself into energetic rubbish, meaning, an item loaded with disorganized energies, polluting the environment and the dwelling where they are stored, thus interfering with the well-being of the people living there (See **Arakaki,** Kátia; *Antibagulhismo Energético* **(Energetic Anti-rubbish)***;* Foz do Iguaçu, PR: *EDITARES;* 2015; p. 33 to 107).

Anti-rubbish. Disposing of energetic knickknacks and rubbish is an antiwastage attitude. Accumulating useful books and knowledge is a prophylaxis against several pathologies of this *Age of Pointless Consumerism.*

2. Obesity. Excessive food intake is one of the main causes of eating disorders, in this case characterized by overweight, morbid obesity. The abundance of food, especially industrialized products, accessible at low prices, has facilitated consciousnesses with some kind of eating disorder, accumulating body fat in a pathological way, with serious risks to somatic health, and repercussions on the personal proexis.

WHO. The World Health Organization (WHO) warns that by 2025, about 2.3 billion adult people will be overweight, and 700 million at risk of becoming obese. The pathology has been growing even in African countries, which is almost paradoxical considering the numerous needs of this continent.

Paradox. The Abundance Society is living the paradox of more people desomating because of an excess of food than because of a shortage of nutrients.

3. Riskomania. Under the label of *entertainment,* adventure tourism, sports, leisure and personal hobbies, all sorts of risky activities proliferate at this beginning of the 21st century. Extreme sports of all kinds become preferred of riskomaniac consciousnesses.

Definition. *Riskomania* is a bad habit, in which people willingly expose themselves to threats to their human existence, or physical and mental integrity, putting themselves time and time again in harms' way in reckless situations of danger, risk, harm, or even death (See **Vieira,** Waldo; Org.; ***Riscomania* (Riskomania); Vieira, *Encyclopaedia of Conscientiology;*** Foz do Iguaçu, PR: *EDITARES / CEAEC;* 8th Ed. Electronic; 2013; p. 9,614 to 9,616).

Rationality. Considering the risks involved in seemingly *innocent* activities, such as trips on ships, theme park tours, mountaineering, and hot air balloon rides, among other forms of entertainments considered "safe", it is worth for an intermissivist reader to rationally assess the risk of a preventable accident. *For those with an existential program, this matter should be taken seriously before pointlessly risking their soma.*

WHILE DEMAND EXISTS FROM THE PATHOLOGIC SOCIN, **POINTLESS** ENERGETIC RUBBISH **WILL CONTINUE** TO BE PRODUCED **ON A LARGE SCALE AND** CONSUMED **BY MILLIONS** OF MISGUIDED CONSCINS UNAWARE OF THEIR OWN EVOLUTION.

Self-questioning. Do you, reading these lines, show any abundance-related pathology? Do you use discernment when choosing activities, thus avoiding unnecessary risks?

11. Syndromes related to Self-wastage

> **Self-dispersiveness.** The greatest problem of the victims of their own versatile talents is **self--dispersiveness** when discarding the essential.[17]

Disorder. A syndrome is a set of symptoms and signs from a group of related causes that, associated, can generate a somatic or mental disorder (See **VandenBos,** Gary R.; Org.; *Dicionário de Psicologia da APA (APA Dictionary of Psychology);* Porto Alegre, RS: *Artmed;* 2010; p. 845).

Syndromes. Waste of the current *Age of Abundance* is also associated to self-wastage syndromes, two of them proposed by this author based on her research on the prevention of self-banalization: the *Self-wastage Syndrome* and the *Ectopic Proexis Syndrome* (See **Manfroi,** Eliana; ***Autopesquisa e Profilaxia da Síndrome da Ectopia de Proéxis* (Self-research and prophylaxis of the Ectopic Proexis Syndrome);** *Annals of the IV Conscientiological Self-research Day;* Florianópolis, SC; *Journal of Conscientiology (JofC);* London; UK: *International Academy of Consciousness* (IAC), 2006; p. 193 to 204). This pathology of *self-dispersiveness* is based on the nosological framework proposed by Vieira (1997).

---

17 **Vieira,** Waldo; *Léxico de Ortopensatas* **(Lexicon of Orthopensatas);** Foz do Iguaçu, PR: *EDITARES;* 2014; p. 194.

Diagnosis. The description of the below syndromes is valid as an warning, without wishing to alarm, and as an attempt to aid in the diagnosis and self-confrontation of such pathologies. Being aware of the problem is the first step to be able to overcome it.

SELF-WASTAGE SYNDROME

Definition. *Self-wastage syndrome* is the pathological condition of the consciousness characterized by the chronic and recurrent personal attitude of squandering and trivializing opportunities, talents, contributions, polyvalences, innate ideas, optimized environments, and notably evolutionary friendships and the *intermissive course* (See **Manfroi,** Eliana; *Síndrome do Autodesperdício* (**Self-wastage Syndrome**); *verbet;* In: **Vieira,** Waldo; Org.; *Encyclopaedia of Conscientiology;* defended at the *CEAEC Tertuliarium,* Foz do Iguaçu, PR, on: 19.05.2014).

Synonymology: 1. *Self-spendthrift Syndrome.* 2. *Self-squandering Syndrome.* 3. Self-wastage Disorder. 4. *Antievolutionary self-wasted Syndrome.* 5. *Self-lossology Syndrome.* 6. Self-trivialization disorder.

Antonymology: 1. Good-use of existential contributions. 2. Self--utilization of strongtraits. 3. Evolutionary non-wastage.

Self-sabotage. We can understand self-wastage from a standpoint of self-sabotage. This is the act of *tricking yourself to stumble and fall, or pulling the rug from under your own two feet.* Self-sabotage is making (or not making) certain choices, preparing the very ground for *everything to go wrong* (See **Stamateas,** Bernardo; *Autossabotagem: Reconheça e mude as Atitudes que você toma contra si mesmo* (**Self-sabotage: recognize and change your attitudes against yourself**); São Paulo, SP: *Academia de Inteligência;* 2009; p. 65 to 84).

Colloquialism. The metaphor of *throwing out the baby with the bath water* appropriately exemplifies the essence of this syndrome. The most important thing, in evolutionary terms, goes *down the drain.*

Symptomatology. Considering the comorbid relations among consciential pathologies, that is, the association of several symptoms or pathologies, we present below 24 symptoms of the *Self-wastage Syndrome:*

01. **Affective ectopy:** misplaced affections; affective immaturity.

02. **Anachronism:** the stance of being an ancestor of oneself.

03. **Antievolutionary inertia:** absence of existential protagonism; writers-block; fear of self-exposure.

04. **Anxiety:** existential anxiety; fluster.

05. **Apriorism:** prejudices; preconceptions about people and ideas.

06. **Blurring:** absence of focus; the fact of being *on the brink of an abyss.*

07. **Consciential dispersion:** self-disorganization; always fully--booked.

08. **Deprioritization:** focus on the superfluous; a superficial posture.

09. **Distortion of reality:** self-deceit; absence of self-realism.

10. **Existential robotization:** sub-cerebral automatism; mediocre existence.

11. **Haste:** superficiality in approaches; treacherous voracity.

12. **Hyperconsumerism:** an excess of junk due to useless collecting.

13. **Impulsiveness:** untimely actions; prejudgments.

14. **Maladjustment:** self-estrangement.

15. **Infantilism:** neoteny; adult or elderly person infantile tantrums.

16. **Mediocrization:** self-levelling by the unthinking and mediocre masses.

17. **Narcissism:** an astonishingly big ego; chronic selfishness.

18. **Perfectionism:** self-justifications; extreme demands.

19. **Procrastination:** always *putting* tasks *off* until *tomorrow*.

20. **Pusillanimity:** giving up without trying; evolutionary cowardice.

21. **Self-sabotage:** self-unworthiness.

22. **Self-sanctification:** defence of one's self-image.

23. **Self-victimization:** self-pity; self-flagellation.

24. **Underestimation:** error of evaluation; the act of thinking small.

Fellowship. Upon losing opportunities of assistance, that is, of helping other consciousnesses, something rather valuable is also lost: our evolutionary companions, our partners, and a group attuned to specific tasks. It is comparable to the situation of a student failing exams, when they see their colleagues and friends moving forward and they stay behind with the "new arrivals", in the condition of an *evolutionary repeater*.

Gauge. The act of measuring, appraising, determining effective wastage hugely helps consciousnesses to pinpoint the drains of some of one's vital personal resources: time, energy, and megafocus.

Self-wastometry. As with the Brazilian *tax-meter*, which measures the annual amount of taxes paid by the Brazilian population, it may be useful for the reader to create a *wastometer* to gauge the level of squandering of existential contributions and evolutionary opportunities occurring.

Self-evaluation. The proposal of an instrument for self-evaluation, in the manner of a *self-wastogram*, has practical utility and can be structured by the reader based on their personal reality.

Self-wastogram. Here is a proposal of a self-assessment inventory, with 10 questions listed in alphabetical order, each related to specific wastage, which can of course be expanded by the reader:

01. **Anxiety.** How many opportunities for self-reflection and being-in-the-moment do I waste by being overly anxious, and occupied with the future (worried)?

02. **Books.** How many books have I failed to read in the past 12 months, even though I have purchased them and *have parked* them in my personal library?

03. **Hobbies.** How much time do I dedicate to a hobby empty of meaning such as collecting beer labels?

04. **Media.** How much time do I spend in front of the TV set watching infantile big audience shows, tearjerker soaps, and listening to dubious quality music?

05. **Net.** How much time do I spend on social media, selecting useful interactivity as opposed to puerile and sometimes self-intruding curiosity?

06. **Self-victimization.** How many opportunities to help do I waste by assuming the role of incapacitated victim, thus reinforcing my low self-esteem?

07. **Shopping.** How many hours do I spend weekly strolling in shopping centres, without a clear purpose, but just *killing time*?

08. **Sleep.** How many hours of sleep do I waste going through hundreds of paid TV channels, filled with *more of the same* completely irrelevant programs?

09. **Soma.** How many physical activities, sometimes even prescribed by a doctor, have I failed to do for lack of organizing my week, thus jeopardizing the welfare of all my vehicles of manifestation?

10. **Texts.** How many texts have I not written due to laziness, procrastination, dispersion, or even intellectual insecurity?

Productivity. By relating the proevolutionary contributions received with the productivity achieved using these resources, it becomes possible to gauge one's own level of wastage. Instead of being a list for self-flagelation, generator of guilt and self-victimization, the relation of self-squandering works as a self-diagnosis indicating the areas, themes, and consciential traits one needs to work on to overcome the *Self-wastage Syndrome*.

Evolution. What is most important, in this period of acceleration in human history, is to identify and diminish the self-wastage of evolutionary inputs. Mismanagement of resources and existential contributions has been generating incalculable deviations and ectopies in our proexes, the theme of the next syndrome.

ECTOPIC PROEXIS SYNDROME

Definition. The *Ectopic Proexis Syndrome,* or syndrome of deviation from one's originally traced evolutionary route, is a pathology characterized by a set of symptoms and related behavioural patterns presented by an ectopic or deviant consciousness, and/or those unsatisfactorily performing their life project (See **Manfroi,** Eliana; *Autopesquisa e Profilaxia da Síndrome da Ectopia de Proéxis* (**Self-research and Prophylaxis from the Ectopic Proexis Syndrome**); *Annals of the IV Conscientiological Self-research Day;* Florianópolis, SC; *Journal of Conscientiology (JofC);* London; UK: *International Academy of Consciousness* (IAC), 2006; p. 193 to 204).

Synonyms. 1. Evolutionary Dysthymia. 2. Proexis Deviation Syndrome. 3. Intraphysical melancholy. 4. Evolutionary failure.

Antonyms. 1. Existential completism. 2. Healthy proexis. 3. Evolutionary success.

Risk. The condition of ectopy, or deviation of one's proexis, may be related to existential anxiety, as already discussed.

Symptomatology. Here are, in alphabetic order, 17 non-exhaustive holosomatic symptoms, also manifested by a conscin with a dysthymic and/or depressive episode, associated with the syndromic frame of an ectopic proexis:

01. **Anhedonia:** the loss of pleasure in performing normally pleasurable activities.

02. **Decidophobia:** chronic indecision; hesitation in choices.

03. **Dispersiveness:** inability to maintain focused attention.

04. **Dysphoria:** dissatisfaction; sadness (dysphoric emotional state).

05. **Euphoria:** exaggerated affective exaltation; exacerbated enthusiasm (euphoric emotional state).

06. **Fatigue:** energetic exhaustion; extreme tiredness.

07. **Guilt:** self-flagellation in face of lost evolutionary opportunities.

08. **Hyperactivity:** impulsive actions; behavioural outbursts.

09. **Hyperappetite:** binge eating generating excessive weight.

10. **Hypersomnia:** the excess of sleep.

11. **Hypoactivity:** excessive immobility; inaction.

12. **Hypoappetite:** lack of appetite generating significant weight loss.

13. **Insomnia:** absence of sleep.

14. **Memory loss:** impaired memory; difficulty in keeping and recovering information.

15. **Self-devaluation:** low self-esteem; a weaktraitist view of yourself; the feeling of uselessness.

16. **Self-exclusion:** conviviality deficit; separation from interactive groups.

17. **Victimization:** blaming others for own existential crisis.

Prophylaxis. The professional training and experience of this author in the area of clinical psychology requires warning the reader to avoid self-application of the list presented without observing the following conditions: if symptoms persist for over 15 days, they should not have been caused (fully or in part) by any prompting episode such as a death in the family, loss of a job, retirement, and other such type of events causing intense but temporary stress, not having a diagnosis of a brain tumour, endocrine dysfunction, or any type of intoxication.

SELF-DISPERSIVENESS SYNDROME

Dispersion. Among the notable characteristics of squandering consciousnesses, dispersion in tasks and self-efforts clearly stands out. The quantity, speed, and instantaneousness of the *novelties* of modern life contribute to *stun* the multifarious consciousness before so many possibilities. Without a megafocus, one wants to go in every direction, and actually goes nowhere.

Syndrome. Vieira identified the *Consciential Dispersion Syndrome* manifested in a large number of disorganized consciousnesses, regarding conscious self-evolution. According to the author, this squandering can lead to poor performance in self-evolution (See **Vieira,** Waldo; ***Temas da Conscienciologia*** (Themes of Conscientiology); Rio de Janeiro, RJ: *IIPC;* 1997; p. 160 and 161).

Definition. The *Consciential Dispersion Syndrome* is the nosological state characterized by a set of signals, symptoms, or traits present in the manifestation of an intermissivist conscin who tends towards disorganization, a lack of mental focus, squandering, deviationism, escapism, subterfuge, and dissipation of efforts in relation to evolutionary prioritizations (See **Cardozo,** Neida; ***Síndrome da Dispersão Consciencial*** (Consciential Dispersion Syndrome); verbet; In: **Vieira;** Waldo; Org.; ***Encyclopaedia of Conscientiology;*** defended at the *CEAEC Tertuliarium,* Foz do Iguaçu, PR, on: 01.08.2014).

Dispersiveness. In this *Age of Abundance* of stimuli, opportunities, invitations, challenges, and novelties, positioning yourself regarding what *not to do* may be the fundamental decision. To disperse efforts by wanting to *embrace the whole world* is the sure path to incompletism, preventing you from finishing your personal evolutionary venture.

Continuism. Sustainability of a priority existential task taken until completion shows the maturity and lucidity of a consciousness regarding priority choices.

Self-deception. A basic consciential trait in the *Consciential Dispersion Syndrome* is deprioritization and this is one of the main symptoms of the carriers of this decision-making disorder.

Symptomatology. Following the self-assessment strategy proposed in this book, here are 9 symptoms manifested by a carrier of this syndrome, in alphabetical order:

1. **Arrogance:** the consciousness does something just because they *can* and *knows* how to, to avoid "loosing" the opportunity, but without evaluating the priority and convergence with their own pre-established goals, thus dispersing themselves.

2. **Carelessness:** lack of zeal and quality in the tasks performed, many times due to the excess of activities assumed, compromising the final result, and generating self and heterofrustration.

3. **Impatience:** immediacy and anxiety can lead the consciousness to assume too much in the short-term, because impatience and lack of perseverance prevent them from sustaining one only, complex, and long-term task, such as writing a book.

4. **Impulsiveness:** the consciousness makes untimely decisions, in an unthinking way, making commitments or wasting resources, even financial ones, in secondary and irrelevant projects.

5. **Pollyannism:** carrier of the *Pollyanna Syndrome,* the consciousness is always ready, happy, and full of energy *for whatever happens,* averaging and seeking to *please all and sundry.*

6. **Resourcefulness:** with an excess of talents and abilities the consciousness can multitask, that is, perform many activities with ease and participate in many fronts of work as *they can take care of everything.*

7. **Self-devaluation:** accepts *any* invitation out of fear of positioning themselves and saying "no", again fearing not meeting expectations and losing the esteem of other consciousnesses due to their own needs and self-underestimation, tending towards dispersivenes in tasks.

8. **Self-disorganization:** absence of a personal agenda, with unstable routine, subject to overloading, without ponderation.

9. **Self-inscience:** absence of self-research and investment in self-awareness, unaware of personal interests and affinities, which are decisive in evolutionary choices.

Poverty. Psychologist and author Daniel Goleman warns of the impoverishment of attention in this *Information Age*. Attention is considered by him as the "cognitive muscle" sustaining human consciousness in the world. Focus and attention when selecting aspects to be included and/or excluded from perception outline the priority reality of each individual (See **Goleman,** Daniel; *Foco: a Atenção e seu Papel Fundamental para o Sucesso* (**Focus: the Hidden Driver of Excellence**); Rio de Janeiro, RJ: *Objetiva;* 2014, p. 81).

Shock. Continually facing intra and extraconsciential distractions, the quality of one´s mental focus, the foundation of antidispersiveness, has been paying a high price in times of excessive stimuli, each struggling to capture and maintain human attention.

Pathology. The difficulty in keeping one´s megafocus on self-determined priority objectives requires overcoming the *Consciential Dispersion Syndrome.*

Multivolous. The trait of a multivolous consciousness, eternally unsatisfied, difficult to please, demanding, wanting everything at once, reinforces antievolutionary dispersiveness (See **Alvarenga;** Bianca: *A Angústia de Fazer Mais e Mais* (**The Anguish of Doing More and More**); *Veja;* São Paulo, SP: *Editora Abril;* 04.05.2016; p. 84 to 87).

THE SYNDROMES ARISING FROM SELF-SQUANDERING VICTIMIZE THE UNAWARE CONSCIOUSNESS AS TO ITS OWN EVOLUTIONARY NORTH, THUS REMAINING LOST AND ECTOPIC REGARDING THE AXIS OF ITS EXISTENTIAL PROGRAM.

Questions. Do you, reader, identify yourself with any of the syndromes presented here? If so, do you accept the challenge to self-confront your own difficulties, without self-victimization?

12. Dormant Proexological Capacity

Dormancy. The seduction of **connectedness** in modern life favours fruitless inertia, notably in the life of disorganized conscins.[18]

Definition. *Dormant proexological capacity* is the deficit between the effective volume of productivity in a consciousness' life program and their real accomplishment potential, planned during intermission, based on personal talents, inputs, and opportunities received (**Manfroi, Eliana;** ***Capacidade Ociosa Proexológica*** (**Proexological Idle Capacity**); *verbet;* In: **Vieira,** Waldo; Org.; ***Encyclopaedia of Conscientiology;***defended at the *CEAEC Tertuliarium,* Foz do Iguaçu, PR: on: 22.01.2014).

Synonyms: 1. Idle proexological capacity. 2. Proexis' unproductive percentage. 3. Proexological lethargy. 4. Balance of debt of one's proexis. 5. Negative difference between what was planned and what was accomplished in a proexis.

Antonyms: 1. Proexological productivity. 2. Proexological usefulness. 3. Up-to-date proexis. 4. Proexological completism.

---

18 **Vieira,** Waldo; ***Léxico de Ortopensatas*** (**Lexicon of Orthopensatas**); Foz do Iguaçu, PR: *EDITARES;* 2014; p. 1,159.

Resource. A dormant or an idle capacity is that resource available for use, but for some reason not actually in use, at a cost for the conscin.

Example. The classroom of a school, when sized for 40 students, but occupied by only 10, has a vacancy rate (or idle capacity) of 75%, considering expenses such as electricity, maintenance and cleaning, depreciation, and mainly payment to teachers, regardless of if they are teaching classes for just a few, or many students.

Proexis. The analogy of the concept applied to one's existential program clarifies the seriousness of neglecting one's own evolution. The question is not if you are doing *a lot,* but rather if you are doing the *fundamental.* A full schedule is not the same as an up-to-date proexis.

Taxology. From the perspective of proexological productivity, here are, in alphabetical order, 8 types of questions related to a consciousness' potential production (proevolutionary antidormancy) followed by most probable dormant, idle and/or neglected skill:

1. **Claritaskal posture.** Do I clarify as much as possible, generating opportunities for claritask? *Idle clarification task.*

2. **Donation of consciential energies.** Do I exteriorize benign energies to all other consciousnesses? *Dormant energosomatic potential.*

3. **Interassistantiality.** Do I do every possible interassistance in my current evolutionary moment? *Dormant fraternism.*

4. **Leadership profile.** Do I inhabit my own leadership profile? *Idle proevolutionary assertiveness.*

5. **Personal talents.** Do I know and make available, to the maximum, my own talents and skills, in an interassistantial way? *Dormant strongtraits.*

6. **Teaching ability.** Am I already teaching what I have learned? *Dormant proevolutionary cognition.*

7. **Welcoming.** Do I express receptivity to other consciousnesses? *Idle welcoming smiles.*

8. **Written production.** Do I frequently write and publish my own self-research, without deficit omissions? *Dormant innate ideas to be transmitted in writing, as in clarifying books kept in drawers.*

Measure. The unit of measure of one´s proexological dormant or idle capacity is *existential emptiness, or void.* We approach this theme in our next chapter.

PROEXOLOGICAL PRODUCTIVITY *IS MEASURED*

BY THE PRIORITIZATION OF WHAT IS ESSENTIAL

BEFORE INTERMISSIVE COMMITMENTS *RATHER THAN*

BY THE AMOUNT OF TASKS LISTED ON ONE´S FULL SCHEDULE.

Self-questioning. What is the balance, reader, between what you have planned and what you have achieved in relation to your own evolutionary life project?

13. Existential Void

> **Excess.** The rhythm of Nature, the **flow of the Cosmos,** and the sequence of existential dimensions can do without *superfluous, exaggeration, excess, waste, futility, extravagance, and void.*[19]

Definition. *Existential void* is the absence of identification or assumption by the consciousness of the meaning of life itself, engendering anguish, anxiety, self-doubt, alienation, depressed mood, and hopelessness in relation to the completion of one's existential program (See **Manfroi;** Eliana; *Vazio Existencial* (**Existential Void**); *verbet;* In: **Vieira,** Waldo; Org.; *Encyclopaedia of Conscientiology;* defended at the *CEAEC Tertuliarium,* Foz do Iguaçu, PR, on: 21.12.2012).

Synonyms: 1. Existential emptiness. 2. Empty proexis. 3. Lack of meaning in life. 4. Existential inequity. 5. Absence of existential purpose. 6. Lack of an evolutionary goal. 7. Intraphysical melancholy.

Antonyms: 1. Sense of life. 2. Existential programming. 3. Evolutionary goal. 4. The purpose of existence. 5. Reason for living. 6. Self-evolutionary goal. 7. Existential plan. 8. Proexological entreprise.

---

19 **Vieira,** Waldo; *Léxico de Ortopensatas* (**Lexicon of Orthopensatas**); Foz do Iguaçu, PR: *EDITARES;* 2014; p. 670.

Disease. The lack of meaning in one's existence constitutes one of the main *existential diseases* of contemporary times. Psychologist practices and religious temples are filled with individuals with this egocentric *complaint.*

Age. French philosopher Gilles Lipovetsky (1944–) calls our attention to an *Age of Void,* and the on-going "individualist revolution" of the 20th and beginning of the 21st centuries, that is, narcissism taken to the ultimate degree in a Society controlled by hedonist and permissive capitalism. He asks if, *under the guise of hypermodernity, is what is essential not escaping through our fingers?* (See **Lipovetsky;** Gilles; *A Era do Vazio* (*L'Ère du Vide: Essais sur l'individualism contemporain* – **The Age of Void: essays on contemporary individualism**); Barueri, SP: *Manole;* 2005; p. 32).

Indifference. Lipovetsky also calls our attention to the phenomenon of historical indifference, the frivolous apathy of individuals who become their own main references (self-centredness), and when they look for themselves they find an empty mirror. *We live in a bunker of indifference,* diagnoses the French philosopher, reflecting what disturbances and existential crises present themselves through this diffuse and invasive malaise of a feeling of inner emptiness.

Apathy. Existential void is closely related to apathy, insensitivity, and indifference in the face of an abundance of possibilities and frivolities in this *Age of Abundance.* What to choose, who to be, what to do, what not to choose, what to identify ourselves with, what to value, what is important, and what is secondary?

Melancholia. Maybe the most recurrent of contemporary faces of this existential void is the process of intraphysical melancholia (*melin*).

Definition. *Melin,* or intraphysical melancholia, is a conscin's morbid state characterized by depression, lack of interest in life, extremely painful state of mind, loss of the capacity to love, even self-love, accompanied by an undefined sadness, and mental and physical abatement, which can result in the manifestation of several psychiatric problems, generally considered more as a phase of manic-depressive psychosis, mood disorder, or bipolar syndrome (See **Vieira**, Waldo; Org.; *Melin; verbet*; *Encyclopaedia of Conscientiology;* Foz do Iguaçu, PR: *EDITARES/CEAEC;* 8th Ed. Electronic; 2013; p. 7,202 to 7,205).

Association. The association between melin and depression requires some caution. Not all depressive symptoms are due to intraphysical melancholia resulting from a deviation of one's existential program. Evaluation by health professionals is always recommended to verify if the mood swing is not due to hormonal causes, brain tumour, or a temporary reactive process, as in an emotional loss, or distress.

Disability. Still, depression is at the top of the list of disorders that most incapacitate individuals for work. Data from the World Health Organization (WHO) show that 7% of the world's population in 2014 (400 million of individuals) suffered with depression, the majority of which of the female gender.

Costs. Researchers tried to calculate the global onus of depression at a seminar held in November 2014 in England, sponsored by *The Economist* magazine, called *The Global Crisis of Depression – The Low of the 21st Century*. Kofi Annan, a former UN secretary-general, announced at the opening of the event that the worldwide cost of depression in 2010 was 800 billion dollars, and that it is expected to double in the next 20 years.

Mega-self-wastage. Severe depression can lead to suicide, which is self-wastage in its maximum expression, denoting megapathology of the consciousness without any lucidity as to the perenniality of consciential principles. It is worth mentioning the fact that *slow indirect suicides* are present in the antisomatic habits and attitudes of contemporary lives of all types of abuse and excess, such as cases of excessive ingestion of alcoholic beverages, smoking, excessive intake of unhealthy foods, and sedentary lifestyle.

Symptoms. Most of the 11 symptoms of depressive disorder, described below in alphabetical order, can also be referred to by consciousnesses who verbalize self-perception of existential emptiness (observe the similarity of the following items with those presented earlier under the *Ectopic Proexis Syndrome* in chapter 10, with the same prophylactic recommendations, of having oneself professionally diagnosed as to the causes of one's depression) (See **Kaplan**, Harold I,; **Sadock**, Benjamin J.; & **Grebb**, Jack A.; ***Compêndio de Psiquiatria: Ciências do Comportamento e Psiquiatrica Clínica*** (**Synopsis of Psychiatry: Behavioural Sciences and Clinical Psychiatry**); Porto Alegre, RS: *Artmed Editora;* 1997; p. 308 and 309):

01. Attention, concentration, and memory disorders.

02. Disinvestment in relationships (isolation).

03. Extreme fatigue.

04. Guilt and anguish.

05. Intense mood swings (intense sadness, inadequate euphoria, extreme anxiety).

06. Loss of interest in pleasurable activities.

07. Low self-esteem.

08. Pessimistic vision of the future (lack of motivation to live).

09. Significant weight oscillation (overweight or underweight).

10. Sleep disorders (hypersomnia or insomnia)

11. Suicidal ideation (in some cases).

Hypothesis. Would the global pandemic of depression not be reinforced by the high incidence of existential emptiness and the lack of meaning of life itself, augmented by chronic indecision in defining our way forward in a society rich in stimuli, but still poor in evolutionary values and cosmoethical principles?

Counterpoints. The following 7 counterpoints synthesize the situation of paradoxical incoherence which permeates the current *Age of Void* (base year: 2016):

1. There have never been *so many contributions* to self-learning and the construction of personal intellectuality, with free access to knowledge, yet there has never been *so little interest* in studying, critical reading, and reflection.

2. There has never been *so much connectivity* between people, through technology and the internet, and yet there has never been *so much superficiality* and absence of deep bonding in relationships.

3. There has never been *so much material abundance*, yet also *so much wastage* in the history of mankind, and even worse, so much *self-wastage*.

4. There has never been *so much investment* in consciousness, in a narcissistic way, and yet *so much self-unawareness* and disorientation regarding one's own identity.

5. There were never *so many opportunities* to help, contribute, be of service to others, by volunteering in an organization, yet there was never *so much emptiness* and lack of meaning in life.

6. There were never *so many possibilities* of professions youngsters can choose from, and yet *so much indecision* about which career to invest in.

7. There was never *so much production* of food in the world, yet *so much need* for nutrients, leading to disease and overeating.

Narcissism. To lead ones' life wholly involved with oneself, prioritizing hedonistic wishes, leads a consciousness to incessantly seek to fill this existential void, paradoxically in that, the more egoic the self-centring, bringing everything to oneself, the emptier of meaning the consciousness becomes.

Addiction. This is a vicious circle in which the loss of the sense of what life is all about makes the consciousness pathologically turn inwards (egocentrism).

Blindness. The visor of individualism blinds a broad vision and prevents the hedonistic consciousness from attaining cosmovision. These are conscins busy only with their own trials and tribulations.

Self-deception. Gross self-corruption and indefensible self-deception reinforce the consciousness' self-devaluation. Even the most egocentric of individuals feels uncomfortable with themselves at some point in their evolution, from the moment they saturate themselves with their own incoherence. The altruists of today were the egocentrics of the past.

Dissatisfaction. Other recurring masks of existential emptiness appear in the form of boredom and indifference. Hyperconsumerism, excessive violence, and the banalisation of life, all common in contemporary times, can have the effect of desensitizing, generating indifference and a lack of empathy for the needs and suffering of others.

Holocaust. Examples of this process of loss of sensitivity to human suffering tend to occur in situations of extreme violence and/or major tragedies. During the Nazi Holocaust, a certain percentage of individuals confined to concentration camps developed a kind of anaesthesia in the face of the on-going barbarism (See **Frankl**, Viktor; *Em Busca de Sentido: Um Psicólogo no Campo de Concentração* (**Man's Search for Meaning: The classic tribute to hope from the Holocaust**); São Leopoldo, RS: *Sinodal & Vozes;* 2008; p. 13).

Sense. Fortunately, not all the victims reached this reactive pathological indifference. Austrian psychiatrist Viktor Emil Frankl (1905–1997), a survivor of a concentration camp, represents one of the best anti-models of this process, by finding meaning for his existence in one of Human History's most brutal episodes.

Logotherapy. Demonstrating an advanced level of resilience, Frankl reports in his books that he only managed to survive the Holocaust by having a reason to stay alive: he wanted to publish his book, whose manuscripts he took to the camp but which were confiscated and destroyed. Sometime after being freed, at the end of World War II, he wrote a book describing his transformative experience, and the principles of logotherapy. The purpose of his life was to help others also find meaning in their lives.

Motivation. The challenge for every lucid consciousness is to find sense for their existence in each new day, as well as motivation for working to fulfil this sense of purpose.

Self-confidence. The feeling of a duty fulfilled before existential demands by means of a useful evolutionary routine avoids any breach for boredom, another symptom arising from existential void.

Boredom. *Boredom* is the feeling of ennui, annoyance, or tiredness caused by something slow, protracted, prolonged, all-encompassing, dry, obtuse or empty, causing undeniable chagrin to a consciousness (See **Vieira**, Waldo; Org; *Tédio* **(Boredom)**; *Encyclopaedia of Conscientiology;* Foz do Iguaçu, PR: *EDITARES/CEAEC;* 8th Ed. Electronic; 2013; p. 10,411 to 10,413).

Motto. The individual who has a reason to live does not waste the opportunity presented by a life in this intraphysical dimension, being unaware of existential boredom.

EXISTENTIAL VOID **IS A PANDEMIC PARAPATHOLOGY OF THIS CURRENT** *AGE OF ABUNDANCE.* **FULL** *LUCID* **REALIZATION OF THE** *MEANING OF LIFE* **CONSTITUTES THE THERAPY AND PROPHYLAXIS FROM MELANCHOLY AND PROEXIC DEVIATION.**

Self-questioning. Have you, reader, already found the evolutionary north of your own intraconsciential compass? Or are you still aimlessly stumbling around, bored by life?

14. Existential Doldrums and the Onus of Self-wastage

Self-stagnation. Your existence is stagnant if you have not, in the last year, changed for the better, at least 5 **personal opinions** on life and consciential evolution.[20]

Doldrumology. Existential doldrums is the condition of being evolutionary *neutral or dead*, in a situation of inertia regarding priority actions concerning your critical current resoma. It is the act of *crossing your arms* before your proexological challenges (See **Manfroi**, Eliana; *Anti-automarasmologia* (**Antidoldrumology**); *verbet;* In: **Vieira**, Waldo; Org.; *Encyclopaedia of Conscientiology;* defended at the *CEAEC Tertuliarium,* Foz do Iguaçu, PR: on: 01.04.2014).

Types. Existential doldrums can assume different forms of consciential manifestation, such as the following 7, listed here in alphabetical order:

1. Self-doldrums in the form of *adaptation.*

2. Self-doldrums in the form of *cowardice.*

3. Self-doldrums in the form of *pride.*

---

20 **Vieira**, Waldo; *Léxico de Ortopensatas* (**Lexicon of Orthopensatas**); Foz do Iguaçu, PR: *EDITARES;* 2014; p. 156.

4. Self-doldrums in the form of *self-deceit*.

5. Self-doldrums in the form of *self-intrusion*.

6. Self-doldrums in the form of *self-reverse*.

7. Self-doldrums in the form of *self-wastage*.

Definition. The *onus of self-wastage* is the cost, price paid, or evolutionary loss absorbed by the unwary consciousness by not positioning themselves before the evolutionary opportunities and existential inputs received.

Synonyms. 1. Onus of spendthriftness. 2. Cost of self-wastage.

Antonyms. 1. Bonus from evolutionary good-use. 2. Existential gains.

Self-wastometer. The following table, with 5 examples, has the didactic function of offering the reader a technique to map out the onus of self-wastage. It begins by relating received inputs, one's reality in relation to its good-use, a calculation in case of loss, and finally an attempt to pinpoint the cause or origin of the self-wastage attitude:

Table – Onus of self-wastage

Nº	Inputs	Reality	Calculated loss	Cause of wastage
1.	Access to books	Poor reader	Scarce intellectuality	Mental laziness
2.	Language learning	Monoglotism	Cultural & interpersonal restriction	Absence of consciential openness
3.	Somatic health	Sedentarism	Fatigue, overweight	Good-timer, self-indulgence
4.	Ease to write	Absence of written production	Dormant capacity to clarify and assist	Dispersiveness, de-prioritization
5.	Network of friends and relationships	Isolation and low social interaction	Solitude and consciential closedness	Egocentrism

Self-discomfort. Surveying self-wastage, as in the above example, can lead the consciousness to experience a kind of *discomfort zone,* which is the intraconsciential condition wherein the individual feels uncomfortable, despondent, annoyed, and restless, with some degree of malaise, insecurity, and dissatisfaction, especially in relation to the incoherent aspects of their self-manifestation, which can paradoxically boost intraconsciential recycling (See **Manfroi,** Eliana; ***Zona de Desconforto* (Discomfort Zone);** *verbet;* In: **Vieira,** Waldo; Org.; ***Encyclopaedia of Conscientiology;*** Foz do Iguaçu, PR: *EDITARES/CEAEC;* 8th Ed. Electronic; 2013; p. 11,019 to 11,023).

Synonyms: 1. No-comfort zone. 2. Self-conflict zone. 3. Intraconsciential itch. 4. Intrapersonal annoyance. 5. Growth crisis. 6. Discomfortology.

Antonyms: 1. Comfort zone. 2. Intimate pacification. 3. Self-nonconflict zone. 4. Comfortology.

Revaluation. The way in which consciousnesses interpret or evaluate facts can be, in a large part, the cause of their annoyance and other unpleasant emotions. Cognitively revaluating one's experiences of self, recycling the way we think, and reducing emotional impact in the face of stressful events minimizes intraconsciential fretting, favouring behavioural changes.

Analogy. Diamond and graphite are simple allotropic substances formed only by the chemical component known as carbon. The difference between them is the coherent atomic structure, cohesive and with few flaws in the case of the valuable sparklers. In an analogy, a *graphite-consciousness* can become a *diamond-consciousness,* by increasing the degree of coherence between thinking, feeling, and acting.

Self-saturation. Among the major causes for entering the discomfort zone is when the consciousness becomes saturated with themselves, overwhelmed by their own incoherent way of thinking, feeling, and acting. This level of cautionary personal discomfort may foreshadow imminent intraconsciential recycling, as the embarrassment can promote dismantling of the previous pattern of manifestation of the self.

Verbaction. Incongruity between *verb* and *action* (verbaction) can provoke self-disturbances and psychological discomforts, such as anxiety, dysthymia, shyness, and/or obsessive disorders. Such symptoms may not be motivated exclusively by the situation of self-incoherence, but they tend to be reinforced by this nosographic intraconsciential condition.

Return. Unwavering encouragement, in both pleasurable and un-pleasant experiences, a focus on what is cost-effective and on serenity, regardless of if the consciousness is in the comfort or discomfort zone may indicate incorruptibility, preceding inner pacification. Each con-sciousness holds the non-transferable power to change itself.

Coherence. The 15 nosographic examples of discomfort zones listed next in alphabetical order, as opposed to a homeostatic condition, can be experienced by consciousnesses still unwary of their own level of coherence. The ability of others to cope with adversity can function as a mirror in which individuals self-evaluate (this is an invitation to the reader):

01. **Anxiety:** anxiety before the anticonflictive posture of others.

02. **Avarice:** the *miserly* before the generous and giving *conscin large.*

03. **Big-Ego:** the egotist before the generosity of other conscious-nesses.

04. **Complaint:** he who complains all the time before the silence of the resolute consciousness.

05. **Corruption:** the corrupt politician before the colleague's cosmoethics.

06. **Defeatism:** the defeatist before their self-motivated evolutionary co-passengers.

07. **Dogmatism:** the *brainwasher* before the independent researcher.

08. **Incomplexis:** the existential incompletist before the successful proexist.

09. **Laziness:** the lazy before the readiness of their evolutionary colleague.

10. **Maladaptation:** the misfit intermissivist vis-a-vis the volunteer of a proevolutionary institution.

11. **Omission:** the unpublished self-researcher before published authors.

12. **Pusillanimity:** the coward before the self-determination of a daring conscin.

13. **Smoking:** the smoker before non-smoking policies.

14. **Victim:** the self-victim before an overcoming resilient consciousness.

15. **Wastage:** the compulsive buyer before the financial intelligence of a saver.

THE DISCOMFORT ZONE EXPERIENCED BY THE INTERMISSIVIST CONSCIN IS A UNIQUE EVOLUTIONARY OPPORTUNITY PROMOTER OF INTRACONSCIENTIAL RECYCLING BASED ON COHERENCE OF SELF-MANIFESTATIONS.

Self-questioning. Do you, reader, consider the possibility of being in a situation of self-wastage? If you feel unsure, we suggest you patiently continue reading this book and its next section, on Antiwastology.

SECTION III
ANTIWASTOLOGY

15. Age of Lucidity

> **Lucidity.** The *unit of measure* of lucidity of an **intermissivist conscin** can be understood as the opportunity to access neoideas and their immediate pratical application, so that the ego may renew itself intraconscientially. If nothing happens after becoming aware of a more advanced idea, this will evidence your so far consolidated evolutionary level.[21]

Definition. *Age of Lucidity* is the period, hypothetically initiated in the last two decades of the 20th century, marked by the emergence of the neoscience conscientiology, characterized by the consciousnesses' discernment regarding their evolutionary priorities, and the assumption of their personal and collective responsibilities concerning the construction of an Educational-Planet, as opposed to a Nosocomial-Planet.

Synonyms: 1. *Age of Discernment.* 2. Cycle of lucidity. 3. *Age of Evolution.*

Antonyms: 1. *Age of Obscurantism.* 2. *Age of Dogmatism.* 3. *Cycle of insanity.*

Cycles. The history of humanity bears evidence of several *ages,* particularly related to geophysical and climatic aspects. The most striking impacts, however, came from milestone ideas, fruitful periods that

---

21 **Vieira,** Waldo; *Léxico de Ortopensatas* (**Lexicon of Orthopensatas**); Foz do Iguaçu, PR: *EDITARES;* 2014; p. 994.

renovated the general mentality, and both individual and collective human thought and behaviour.

Lucidity. Lucidity can also be understood as the interval of sanity, mental hygiene between periods of mental confusion and the obnubilation of discernment. Among the pathological or immature periods of human societies recorded by History, there were moments of greater rationality and common sense, influencing the following stages and propelling evolution in the world.

Counterpoint. Conscientiology emerges at the height of contemporary materialism and capitalism, as an antidogmatic and antiwasteful counterpoint to the trivialization of evolutionary time and still neglected existential opportunities.

Disorientation. Domenico de Masi takes us in an exhaustive journey through the main models of life that have guided Humanity since Antiquity, in his book *Il futuro è arrivato,* published in Brazil in 2014 under the title *O Futuro Chegou: Modelos de Vida para uma Sociedade Desorientad* (The Future Has Arrived: Lifestyles for a Disoriented Society). In the analysis of what he calls a *post-industrial model,* he argues that human society is professing a single rite – consumption; a single moral – that of *never having enough* and that there *is never too much abuse.* For the author, the model under analysis wallows in the superfluous, reflecting the absence of lucidity regarding an opportunity for a pro-evolutionary paradigmatic change in this beginning of the 21st century (See **Masi,** Domenico de; ***O Futuro Chegou: Modelos de Vida para uma Sociedade Desorientada*** (The Future Has Arrived: Lifestyles for a Disoriented Society); Rio de Janeiro, RJ: *Casa da Palavra;* 2014; p. 590).

Milestones. It is worth reflecting on these 9 Western civilizing ideational milestones, 5 amplifiers, and 4 reducers of consciential lucidity, listed in chronological order and classified into 2 distinct groups:

A. **Amplifiers:**

1. Hellenism – Ancient Greece (centuries III to I b.c.e).

2. Roman Classicism (II century b.c.e).

3. Renaissance (XV to XVII centuries).

4. Enlightenment (XVIII century).

5. Conscientiology (XX century onwards).

B. **Reducers:**

6. Feudalism (centuries V to XV).

7. Monarchical absolutism.

8. Totalitarianism.

9. Religious fundamentalism.

Antigenuflection. Religious dogmatism, in its many forms, in any historical period, has presented itself as one of consciousnesses main reducers of self-discernment. The *Age of Lucidity,* when implanted in its fullness, will demarcate the end of the ideological genuflection imposed by alienating religions.

Evidence. Some evidence of the current *Age of Lucidity* can already be perceived in these two first decades of the 21st century, like the following 29 listed here in alphabetical order:

01. Amnesty International's movement.

02. Drop in illiteracy rates and increase in the general level of literacy.

03. Eradication of disease and improvement in the general condition of entire populations.

04. Extending human ethics to cosmoethics.

05. Extending law to paralaw.

06. Formation of the *International Cosmoethical Conscientiological Community* (ICCC).

07. Growing community work initiatives for improving the quality of life.

08. Growth of freedom of expression in all media.

09. Implementation of specific localities aiming at propelling evolution, such as new *cities of knowledge (Cognopolis).*

10. Institutions focused on the betterment of consciousness as a whole *(Conscientiocentric Institutions).*

11. International conventions on all sorts of consciential discrimination.

12. International conventions on war refugees, hunger and oppression.

13. International mine-clearance agreements (landmine bans).

14. International movement for the rejection of violence and implementation of a *Culture of Peace.*

15. International movement for voluntary work.

16. International movements for animal rights.

17. International movements for conscious and sustainable consumption.

18. International movements for the end of slavery.

19. International movements for the eradication of poverty.

20. International protocols for the prevention of international people trafficking.

21. International treaties banning nuclear tests.

22. Libraries, encyclopaedias, and books accessible to the public for free.

23. Non-governmental humanitarian aid organizations, such as *Médecins Sans Frontières (Doctors without Borders)*.

24. Planetary connection through the *World Wide Web*.

25. Proposition of edification of the World State[22].

26. Sharp decline in infant mortality.

27. Significant drop in tobacco consumption (smoking) across the planet.

28. *The Principle of Disbelief,* proposed by the science conscientiology, as an antidogma vaccine for absolute truths from religious, political, scientific, or philosophical nature.

29. Writing of collective, open and voluntary books, such as the *Encyclopaedia of Conscientiology.*

Axiology. It is important to understand the evolutionary values of consciential self-lucidity and self-coherence manifest in antiwastage attitudes. In this *Age of Lucidity* the conditions considered favourable to Intraphysical Society, still disoriented, do not serve human evolution,

---

22 The *World State* is the policy of universalist cooperation, interchange, and integration between nations, a conquest made possible by technological advancement, and the inevitable consensus of gradual homogenization of laws and rules governing such a regime, respecting individual or cultural rights of any given population (V. **Vieira,** Waldo, ***Homo sapiens pacificus;*** Foz do Iguaçu, PR, 2007; *CEAEC;* p. 798).

without the maximum possible use of discernment. *Anti-self-wastage is self-discernment.*

IN THIS AGE OF LUCIDITY, SELF-WASTAGE CAN BE ERADICATED THROUGH PRIORITIZATION BY A DISCERNING CONSCIOUSNESS AWARE OF ITS COMMITMENTS, ASSUMED IN THE FACE OF THE INTERASSISTANTIAL DEMANDS OF THIS HOSPITAL-PLANET.

Self-questioning. Do you, the reader, have enough discernment regarding whether this is your most lucid existence in the entire sequence of rebirths? What evolutionary gains are you deriving from that fact?

16. Prophylaxis from Self-wastage

Self-wastage. The worst waste of the human personality is that of idle theorical **self-cognition**, without greater cosmoethical evolutionary application.[23]

Definition. *Prophylaxis from self-wastage* is a technique or set of attitudes, postures, behaviours, choices, prioritizations, decisions, intentions, and procedures adopted by the lucid consciousness actively avoiding the waste of opportunities, strongtraits, abilities, intelligences, genialities, innate ideas, relationships, *reencounters of destiny,* and existential inputs, catalysers of the execution of one's personal and collective existential program (**Manfroi,** Eliana; *Evitação do Autodesperdício* (**Avoidance of Self-wastage**); *verbet;* In: **Vieira,** Waldo; Org.; *Encyclopaedia of Conscientiology;* Foz do Iguaçu, PR: *EDITARES/CEAEC;* 8th Ed. Electronic; 2013; p. 4,855 to 4,860).

Synonyms: 1. Evolutionary self-non-wastage. 2. Prophylaxis from self-squandering. 3. Applied *evolutionary intelligence.* 4. Avoidance of self-sabotage; prevention of self-deceit.

Antonyms: 1. Wastage of strongtraits. 2. Consciential ectopy. 3. Self-avarice. 4. Existential self-boycott. 5. Crass self-deception. 6. Self-intrusion.

---

23 **Vieira,** Waldo; *Léxico de Ortopensatas* (**Lexicon of Orthopensatas**); Foz do Iguaçu, PR: *EDITARES;* 2014; p. 184.

Colloquialism. Some popular expressions or idioms can translate well the self-wastage process: *scoring an own-goal; missing the train of history; pulling the rug from under one's own feet; tripping on one's own feet; shooting yourself in the foot.*

Precision. On the other hand, there are expressions that synthesize the exact contrary idea: *not losing the thread* of one's own life project; *being on the ball* regarding evolutionary choices; *acting on the fly* as to the essence of one's existential program.

Intelligence. The fact that one does not engage in self-wastage evidences a reasonable degree of *evolutionary intelligence* of the consciousness. The level of this intelligence transpires in its evolutionary priorities, given the lucid choices of what is actually relevant.

Discard. In thesis, it is very difficult for a consciousness to be able to seize every opportunity coming their way. The *touch* of evolutionary genius is precisely in knowing what to discard, without attachments and dramas.

Self-positioning. Electing something as a priority requires, at the same time, giving up on countless other possibilities. It is about paying the price for deciding what is more relevant, detaching yourself from all else, but in-sight of perceived evolutionary gains. This is the *bonus of 'No'*: what you *gain* by *losing* something (**Teles,** Mabel; ***Bônus do Não*** (**The Bonus of No**); *verbet;* In: **Vieira,** Waldo; Org.; ***Encyclopaedia of Conscientiology;*** Foz do Iguaçu, PR: *EDITARES/CEAEC;* 8th Ed. Electronic; 2013; p. 2,535 to 2,539).

Example. To help in understanding the practical meaning of *the bonus of 'No'*, it is worth offering some examples. In Conscientiology, the expression *ideological maxidissidence* means the lucid choice a consciousness makes when giving up an indoctrinating, sectarian, and oppressive group, in favour of a liberating and anti-dogmatic ideology, as when a former fanatic person abandons an antiuniversalistic institution.

Case-study. A classic example is the case of a radical political militant leaving partisan extremism in favour of voluntary work in an institution focused on free thinking and proevolutionary consciential openness.

Dismissal. Another case of illustrative examples are a consciousness' *cosmoethical foibles,* or practice of seemingly retreating, declining, or ousting something in favour of self and hetero-evolution. A good example of proevolutionary ousting is when a consciousness relinquishes positions of power and accumulation of money when these represent risks to self-cosmoethics.

Megaprevention. Lack of lucidity in the face of the *trinomial sex-power-money* is responsible for the collapse of civilizations and individuals throughout recorded Human History. In contemporaneity, this trinomial is still exerting lethal effects over too many consciousnesses oblivious to the seductions of such pseudo-pleasures. A lucid and determined consciousness, guided by their recognized evolutionary north-star, uses the force of their unbreakable will to overcome the secular seduction of the aforementioned trinomial.

Anticipation. Conscientiology has been thoroughly researching the mega-prophylactic measures to the *sex-power-money* triad. Among the various available techniques is the trinomial composed of 3 complementary strategies: *existential inversion–evolutionary duo–personal energetic task,* evidencing the advantages of this neoscience in relation to other lines of study of consciousness.

Inversion. The *existential inversion technique,* or invexis, can be summarised as the intelligent anticipation of useful productivity in the existence of a consciousness from youth, through the maximum planning of their human life aiming at existential completism. Consisting of calculated proevolutionary choices, invexis constitutes one of the main measures of self-wastage prophylaxis (See **Nonato,** Alexandre; *et. al.; Inversão Existencial: Autoconhecimento, Assistência e Evolução desde a Juventude* (**Existential Inversion: Self-awareness, Assistance, and Evolution since Youth**); *Editares;* 2011; p. 22 to 42).

Requirements. Existential inversion constitutes one of the most advanced evolutionary strategies in conscientiology, and perhaps due to its complexity, also one of the most controversial. It is worth highlighting here some of the items the young candidates for the application of this technique will need to face, such as: the lucid choice of not having children, as this fact entails a commitment to the resomating consciousness for at least the first 18 years of life; the lucid choice of avoiding abortion, preventing self-guilt and karmic interprisons; the lucid choice of not effecting civil or religious marriage, but rather seeking to apply the *evolutionary duo technique,* as described below; the lucid choice of not using licit and illicit drugs due to the harmful consequences of such a habit (See **Nonato,** Alexandre; *et. al.; Inversão Existencial: Autoconhecimento, Assistência e Evolução desde a Juventude* (**Existential Inversion: Self-awareness, Assistance, and Evolution since Youth**); Foz do Iguaçu, PR: *Editares;* 2011; p. 50 and 51).

Evolutionary-duo. The *evolutionary duo technique* is the lucid pairing of a man and a woman who consciously waive conventional expectations about life as a couple, such as a formal marriage and children, to optimize their own evolution to the maximum, initiating interassistance by assisting each other in the intimacy of their own home. It is one of the main prophylactic measures for immature sexuality and emotional need (**Vieira,** Waldo; ***Manual da Dupla Evolutiva*** (**Evolutionary Duo Manual**); Rio de Janeiro, RJ: *IIPC;* 1997; p. 10 to 168).

Penta. *Personal energetic task,* in short, penta, is the daily commitment assumed by a consciousness to exteriorize homeostatic energies, acting jointly with extraphysical helpers, without any mysticism or rituals, assisting whoever is in need, whether they be conscins or consciexes.

Network. This is anonymous help, carried out by the person in an environment where they alone are present, in intraphysical terms, but that has an extensive network of auxiliaries from an ample extraphysical team. It is a task undertaken for the rest of one's human life, where the assistant provides their own healing energies and personal balance to help other consciousnesses so they can also enjoy this condition, which is fundamental in efforts of self-renewal (**Waldo,** Vieira; *Manual da Tenepes* **(Penta Manual)**; Rio de Janeiro, RJ: *IIPC;* 1995; p. 11).

Deepening. We would recommend to a reader interested in deepening their research on such advanced techniques to read some published conscientiological works, notably the manuals indicated in the bibliography.

Disclaimer. This book is not intended to stimulate or generate a *syndrome of urgency,* as if the planet was about to end tomorrow and everything needs to be solved *today.* To avoid anxiety about evolutionary choices is to avoid gross mistakes in the very conduct of one's existence (See **Vieira,** Waldo; *Dicionário de Argumentos da Conscienciologia* **(Dictionary of Conscientiology Arguments)**; Foz do Iguaçu, PR: *EDITARES;* 2014; p. 127).

Steps. Every journey starts with a first step, and so the long journey towards self-awareness also follows this precept. In life's essential undertakings careful consideration and discernment are essential companions.

Haste. Excessive simultaneous activity is probably one of the causes for self-wastage. Existential anxiety is the shortest path to a lack of achievement. In such cases, there is a false sense of producing a lot, but the actual results are minimal and pulverized.

Build-up. Avoidance of self-wastage is a style of consciential manifestation that requires the consciousness' daily care, gradually implementing small precautionary measures with significant cumulative results. The *evolutionary useful day technique* attends to this need.

EVOLUTIONARY USEFUL DAY TECHNIQUE

Technicality. The *evolutionary useful day technique* is the daily strategy of taking advantage of each new daily opportunity to develop 3 aspects considered essential in a truly productive 24 hours:

1. **Cognition:** learn something new (neolearning), *every day.*

2. **Interassistance:** help someone, or yourself (neoassistance), *every day.*

3. **Production:** produce useful written neoideas (neoproductivity), *every day.*

Sequence. Self-prescriptive, this *technique* is developed using a 3-step sequence, described below in functional order. It is worth highlighting here the importance of balancing the implementation of the proposed steps, so as to avoid carrying out only one of the steps and neglecting the others. Here are the steps:

Step 1 – Neolearning. Diarize your days allocating time for critical reading, study, and research of useful sources. It is worth observing other sources of neocognition, such as conversations and exchanges of useful ideas with other people; visits to bookshops and libraries; attending courses and lectures; research trips. *Tips:* record as much as possible of the new ideas coming from your daily cognitive activities; organize your intellectual workplace by creating a space favourable to neocognitions; self-reflection is also neolearning.

Step 2 – Neoassistance. Organize your diary allocating daily time for some type of advanced interassistance, such as voluntary work in a proevolutionary institution, voluntary clarification teachings, daily donation of healthy energies at a pre-arranged schedule (penta), among others. *Tip:* stay alert to extra non-scheduled interassistantial needs, notably those of a multidimensional nature.

Step 3 – Neoproductivity. Organize your diary preferably allocating daily time for writing, whether accounts of experiences, articles, books, and/or courses, among other modalities. *Tip:* try to surround yourself with books and reference materials, such as dictionaries, encyclopaedias, technical treatises, and digital information.

Myth. The idea that self-organization and useful routines *stifle* creativity and heuristic production is a contemporary myth and its days are numbered. Original productivity by a disciplined consciousness is, in most cases, higher and of a better quality than that of disorganized individuals expecting 99% of inspiration without even 1% of perspiration.

Flexibility. Rigidity and inflexibility are not synonyms of discipline and organization, be that intraphysical or mentalsomatic. Openness to new ideas and original inspirations enhances intellectual parapsychism (See **Vieira,** Waldo; Org.; ***Parapsiquismo Intelectual*** **(Intellectual Parapsychism)**; ***Encyclopaedia of Conscientiology;*** *EDITARES/CEAEC;* 8th Ed. Electronic; 2013; p. 8,138 to 8,141).

Every-day-life. Existential completism is the result of daily mini-completism. The analysis of an individual´s single day can provide evidence of the tendencies of an entire lifetime. An aware intermissivist seeks self-organization to experience a week of *7 evolutionarily useful days.*

*AVOIDANCE OF SELF-WASTAGE IS A **PRIORITY COMMITMENT FOR A LUCID CONSCIOUSNESS RESPONSIBLE FOR** DISTINGUISHING WHAT IS WORTHLESS **FROM THE ESSENTIAL, WHAT IS IRRELEVANT FROM THE NECESSARY, AND WHAT IS OBSOLETE** FROM THE EVOLUTIONARY.*

Self-questioning. Would you consider applying prophylactic techniques against self-wastage? Have you already thought about creating your own proevolutionary techniques and publishing these strategies anytime soon? (Here is another tip).

17. Avoidance of Autobsolescence

> **Intolerance.** Intolerance is one of the major human irrationalities as it implies squandering evolutionary opportunities in block. Yet, we should not stay paralyzed before obsolescence and we need to strive for new evolutionary ideas.[24]

Definition. *Avoidance of autobsolescence* is the act or effect by which an aware consciousness updates their way of thinking evolution-wise, their self-manifestation, and their existential *curriculum*, avoiding the anachronistic condition of becoming the ancestor of oneself (See **Manfroi**, Eliana; ***Evitação da Autobsolescência*** (**Avoidance of Autobsolescence**); verbet; In: **Vieira**, Waldo; Org.; ***Encyclopaedia of Conscientiology;*** defended at the *CEAC Tertuliarium,* Foz do Iguaçu, PR, on: 16.06.2015).

Synonyms: 1. Prophylaxis from autobsolescence. 2. Avoidance of self-anachronism. 3. Avoidance of self-conservatism. 4. Prevention of self-fossilization. 5. Overcoming self-outdatedness.

Antonyms: 1. Autobsolescence. 2. Auto-anachronism. 3. Auto--archaism.

---

24 **Vieira**, Waldo; ***Léxico de Ortopensatas*** (**Lexicon of Orthopensatas**); Foz do Iguaçu, PR: *EDITARES;* 2014; p. 917.

Autobsoleteness. Considered as one of the less obvious faces of the self-destructive profile, autobsoleteness manifests itself mainly in the ideational area, that is, in an obsolete way of thinking and acting.

Mimesis. Contemporary examples of people and groups who seek to reproduce the medieval way of life, for instance, by dressing and living in similar conditions, can illustrate this type of existential ectopy. In Conscientiology, this process is called dispensable self-mimesis.

Counterproductiveness. Vieira accurately defines this condition of autobsolescence thus in the homonymic verbet: "*Ancestor of oneself* is the consciousness *whose past has not yet passed,* and who is trying to live today unconsciously repeating everything already *done and dusted* in several previous human lives (seriexology), by means of already *dispensable self-mimesis,* inconvenient and counterproductive for consciential evolution itself*"* (**Vieira,** Waldo; Org.; ***Antepassado de Si Mesmo*** (**Ancestor of Oneself**); ***Encyclopaedia of Conscientiology;*** Foz do Iguaçu, PR: *EDITARES/ CEAEC;* 8th Ed. Electronic; 2013; p. 650 to 655).

Revival. To manifest oneself in the present life with the same mentality and attitudes of past existences is to waste opportunities for renewal and evolutionary updates. Such a consciousness is *treading water,* or just *walking around in circles* in relation to the demands of recycling in this *Age of Lucidity.* Autobsoleteness is self-wastage.

Self-assessment. It is rather important for the self-waster to diagnose their own obsolescence levels by means of doing an honest self-assessment, and examination the presence of the following 19 obsolete but still quite current consciential manifestations, listed in alphabetical order:

01. **Bellicosity:** verbal and physical violence; exaggerated competitiveness.

02. **Childishness**: infantile desires and temper tantrums in a grown adult.

03. **Conservatism**: phobia of the new and of self-renewing changes.

04. **Consumerism**: the irrationality of acquiring unnecessary items.

05. **Dogmatism**: concepts taken as absolute truths.

06. **Homophobia**: spurious prejudices; puritan and anachronistic morals.

07. **Illiteracy**: as in the absence of minimal erudition and cognition.

08. **Interiorosis**: life restricted to one's *internal little world* of ideas and minimal conviviality.

09. **Irritability**: irascible behaviour, intolerant of any frustration.

10. **Monarchism**: despotic postures, boasting, and subjugation of others.

11. **Monoglotism**: poverty in intercommunication due to only speaking one's mother tongue.

12. **Partisanship**: the absence of intelligent *hovering-above*, opting instead for reductionist factions.

13. **Polycomplaintiveness**: endless complaints and looking for favouritisms.

14. **Radicalism**: a one-track mind supporting extreme and excluding positions.

15. **Religiousness**: ideational genuflection and uncritical enslavement to religious dogma.

16. **Sexism:** ignorance regarding the condition of the consciousness, essentially, being asexual, manifesting sometimes in a feminine and at other times in a masculine soma.

17. **Stubbornness:** absence of minimal self-criticism, and resistance to self-recycling.

18. **Bifrontism:** inauthenticity; concealment; manipulation.

19. **Victimization:** personal posture as a *victim of the entire universe.*

Multiexistentiality. Based on the principle of a consciousness' multiple existences, it is possible to understand the continuity of certain activities or behaviours from the past still manifesting in one's current life. However, it becomes urgent to evaluate if such recurrence is a strongtrait or a weaktrait of that consciousness, the latter characterizing antievolutionary self-mimesis. The comparison proposed below is intended to aid self-reflection on this subject.

Confrontology. Under the optics of *comparology,* here are, for example, 9 aspects of stagnating retrolives compared with a new manifestation that propels self-evolution, in alphabetic order:

1. **Authorship:** in the *past,* a writer of literature; in the *present,* an author of a technical work.

2. **Countenance:** in the *past,* a frowning face; in the *present,* a sincere smile.

3. **Elocution:** in the *past,* opportunistic eloquence; in the *present,* cosmoethical debatology.

4. **Evolutionary-partnership:** in the *past,* irresponsible promiscuity; in the *present,* a partner in an emotionally successful evolutionary duo.

5. **Expression:** in the *past,* self-repressed communication; in the *present,* didactic histrionics.

6. **Politics:** in the *past,* manipulative demagogy; in the *present,* a democratic consciousness.

7. **Posture:** in the *past,* the vow of poverty; in the *present,* the experience of complex frugality.

8. **Psychosoma:** in the *past,* the primacy of art; in the *present,* a mentalsomatic megafocus.

9. **Task:** in the *past,* religious assistance; in the *present,* claritaskal volunteering.

Priority. Maintaining evolutionary priorities up-to-date is a prophylaxis against autobsolescence. Nevertheless, it is intelligent, from the point of view of Evolutiology, to evaluate new demands in relation to one's already established priorities, and if necessary to resist unnecessary changes.

Avoidance of autobsolescence **is an essential clause in the evolutionary agenda of any consciousness motivated to** *recycle and acquire neopostures* **in the consciential paradigm.**

Self-questioning. Have you, reader, been recycling obsolete and anachronic consciential traits? Which preventative strategies do you use to avoid becoming a *museum piece?*

18. Prudent Audacity

Audacity. In theory, **audacity** is preferable to *pusillanimity* in proexological ventures. *If you do not dare you do not lose, but neither do you win.*[25]

Definology. *Prudent audacity* is the aptitude or healthy straightforward manifestation of associating boldness, audacity, with ponderation, sensibility, and rationality in one's own attitudes, positions, and evolutionary choices (See **Manfroi,** Eliana; *Audácia Prudente* (**Prudent Audacity**); *verbet;* In: **Vieira,** Waldo; Org.; *Encyclopaedia of Conscientiology;* defended at the *CEAEC Tertuliarium,* Foz do Iguaçu, PR, on: 14.02.2014).

Synonyms: 1. Judicious boldness. 2. Cautious courage. 3. Premeditated daring 4. Discerning courage. 5. Calculated bravery. 6. Prudent fearlessness. 7. Justified audacity.

Antonyms: 1. Imprudent audacity. 2. Thoughtless daring. 3. Foolish courage. 4. Unthinking fearlessness. 5. Uncritical impulsivity.

Evolution. Seeking evolutionary acceleration requires a certain amount of existential boldness on the part of the lucid consciousness. However, audacity in the face of challenges and new opportunities requires a high dosage of wisdom and rationality. Lucid temperance is indicative of *evolutionary intelligence.* Knowing when to move forward,

---

25 **Vieira,** Waldo; *Léxico de Ortopensatas* (**Lexicon of Orthopensatas**); Foz do Iguaçu, PR: *EDITARES;* 2014; p. 149.

retreat, or wait, in the face of a critical situation, characterizes prudent audacity.

Riskomania. To waste the evolutionary opportunity of living by risking your one essential tool in this dimension, the human body, is recurrent in this *Age of Abundance* of extreme sports, violent entertainment, adrenaline addiction, and naive disengagement with evolution itself.

Naivety. Even touristic activities considered "innocent" can put one's soma at risk of early aborting the consciousness' life project. How many tourists lose their lives, for example, on boat trips in places with precarious safety, on hot air balloon flights, *rappelling* or abseiling in dangerous so-called natural paradises, foolish mountaineering, among so many other pseudo-amusements, already referred to in chapter 10.

Self-discernment. By rationally evaluating the importance and commitment of longevity useful for the execution of one's existential program, it is worth reflecting on the exercise of professional activities, as in the case of journalists covering war conflicts, or even volunteers of humanitarian causes in risky areas.

Boldness. An example of calculated boldness is that of a middle-aged person (40 to 65 years of age), giving up their *golden handcuffs* in favour of claritaskal volunteering, a situation considered a *waste* from the perspective of intraphysical society, but probably indicating an optimal use of one's life. Needless to say, in order to give up one's "dream" job, the individual must have put together their proexogenic savings, that is, the financial resources capable of maintaining dignified self-sustainability.

Resilience. Another unique aspect of prudent audacity is the fact that setbacks can strengthen a consciousness, rendering it resilient before adversity.

Self-intrusionology. From the standpoint of *Antiexamplogy*, here are examples of 8 consciential profiles classified into 2 groups: *audaciously imprudent* and *audaciously prudent* consciousnesses.

A. **Audaciously imprudent:**

1. **Activist.** Women's civil rights militant in direct confrontation with radical leaders of a misogynist country.

2. **Diplomat.** Diplomatic High Commissioner risking their own life on a diplomatic mission in a war zone.

3. **Environmentalist.** Volunteer of an international environmental organization invading state facilities guarded by armed security.

4. **Journalist.** Reporter covering an armed conflict directly from the battle *front*.

B. **Audaciously prudent:**

5. **Leader.** Cosmoethical leadership, a resomatic attractor pondering the suitable contexts where to expose advanced ideas (verpons).

6. **Scientist.** A scientist and thinker of the past denying their own advanced discovery to preserve life and continuing researching.

7. **Parapsychic.** The master paraperceptiologist camouflaging leading-edge parapsychic extrapolations, waiting for the formation of a consciential critical mass capable of understanding the contents of the phenomena.

8. **Writer.** The author of controversial subject giving up on the immediate publication of a text, and waiting for the right moment for divulgation, avoiding any risk to their physical integrity.

*PRUDENT AUDACITY **EVIDENCES THE LEVEL OF MATURITY OF A CONSCIOUSNESS AS TO** COSMOETHICALLY CALCULATED EXISTENTIAL BOLDNESS, **AND EVOLUTIONARY INTELLIGENCE WHEN EVALUATING THE** PRIORITY OF THE CHALLENGES.*

Self-questioning. Have you, reader, been using prudent audacity before the megachallenges of your evolution? Can you already distinguish between the act of performing *blind flights* and the act of walking safely even on an *inhospitable path*?

19. The Onus of Difference

Differentiation. Culture, intellectuality, self-awareness, erudition, or polymathy is what more differenti-
ates, or sets **human beings** apart from each other.[26]

Definition. The *onus of difference* is the price a lucid intermissivist
conscin needs to pay for transcending or going beyond the level of mediocrity of their evolutionary group, manifesting qualitatively differentiated and extemporaneous cognition, behaviour, and stance regarding the
holothosene of the existing *zeitgeist* (See **Manfroi,** Eliana; Ônus da Diferença
(**Onus of Difference**); *verbet;* In: **Vieira,** Waldo; Org.; *Encyclopaedia of Conscientiology;* presented at the *CEAEC Tertuliarium,* Foz do Iguaçu, PR, on: 01.10.2013).

Synonyms: 1. The price of singularity. 2. The cost of diversity.
3. The toll of dissimilarity. 4. The value of non-uniformity. 5. The tax for
authenticity. 6. The burden of consciential singularity. 7. The onus of
intermissivist innate ideas.

Antonyms: 1. Equality bonus. 2. Benefit of similarity. 3. Onus of
consciential equitability.

Colloquiology. The colloquial idiom *swimming against the tide*
exemplifies the very essence of the *onus of difference.*

---

26 **Vieira,** Waldo; *Léxico de Ortopensatas* (**Lexicon of Orthopensatas**); Foz do
Iguaçu, PR: *EDITARES;* 2014; p. 527.

Remark. It is worth alerting the reader to the fact that such a posture is different from the arrogance or prepotency of considering intermissivists "special people" or "distinctive beings" before the inalienable right of every consciousness to evolve. It is, above all, a question of realism and self-awareness of the differentiated condition of those who decide to evolve and not be wasted, against all the odds on this Hospital-Planet.

Dissidence. Decisions made by some consciousnesses, which pay the price of proevolutionary differentiation, can generate misunderstandings in familiar and convivial groups.

Maxidissidence. An example of this fact is the already mentioned condition of *conscientiological maxidissidence*, when a person voluntarily leaves their initial convivial group, as the latter reveals itself incoherent with the individual's new evolutionary values, or when the individual becomes aware of the stagnant, anticosmoethical *socialite* aspects of such conviviality (See **Luz,** Marcelo da; ***Onde a Religião Termina? (Where Does Religion End?)***; Foz do Iguaçu, PR: *Editares;* 2011; p. 19 to 28).

Onus. An authentic consciousness pays the price of displeasing many co-passengers. To give up responding to the expectations of other consciousnesses is the mark of an antisquanderer. Warning: consciential authenticity is not the same as verbal aggressiveness or an absence of *evolutionary etiquette.*

Outlander. The condition of feeling like a "stranger in the nest", different from the standards of the closest convivial group, may lead some individuals to give up their own uniqueness to be accepted by other consciousnesses. When this happens and the condition lasts for a long period, there is an elevated chance of self-wastage.

Talents. An example of this is the case of the consciousness with multiple talents and capacities, "strikingly different" from their family, school colleagues, and friends, "covering-up" their strongtraits to avoid being excluded or feeling marginalized. A consciousness' strongtraits can bother others more than their weaktraits, leading to the paradoxical situation of self-repression of one's own abilities, many of which were acquired and polished in successive retrolives.

Accountancy. Here are, for example, in alphabetical order, 7 different *prices* to be paid by an anti-squandering consciousness in this *Age of Abundance*:

1. The *cost* of a differentiated stance in the midst of surrounding mediocrity.

2. The *cost* of a growth crisis in plain comfort zone.

3. The *cost* of a surplus omission in the face of narcissistic overexposure.

4. The *cost* of assuming one's evolutionary level as opposed to hiding deficit omissions.

5. The *cost* of dissidence from eletronotic science by the self-researcher.

6. The *cost* of intraconsciential recycling as opposed to sameness.

7. The *cost* of relative truths experienced in face of stagnating mimicry.

Parahistoriology. From the point of view of *invulgarology,* there are innumerable different historical personalities who were burdened by their advanced ideas and behaviours, such as the philosopher and mathematician Hypatia of Alexandria (370–451), victimized by misogynists and religious fanatics; and the young Italian scholar and philosopher Giovanni Pico Della Mirandola (1463–1494), accused of heresy by his Catholic detractors.

Conviviology. The savvy intermissivist seeks to interact and integrate socin and their co-passengers, conscious of their own interassistantial role, and of the importance of orthoconviviality. They avoid, as best as possible but without antievolutionary concessions, to be an *avis rara* or *weirdo,* although they can differ by their cosmoethically-qualified *modus operandi.*

Lucidology. According to *self-lucidology,* for example, here are in alphabetic order 9 conscientiological specialities followed by traits and/or differentiated consciential postures capable of generating an onus of difference, but at the same time predisposing the intermissivist to receiving an evolutionary bonus:

1. **Claritaskology.** Impactotherapeutic interlocution *predisposing* claritaskal interassistance.

2. **Disbeliefology.** Explicit antidogmatism *predisposing* ideational autonomy.

3. **Exemplogy.** Leveraging incorruptibility *predisposing* staggering exemplarism.

4. **Neophiliology.** Continued neophilia *predisposing* consciential openness.

5. **Prioritariology.** Evolutionary radicalism *predisposing* existential prioritization.

6. **Proexology.** Proexic self-coherence *predisposing* existential completism.

7. **Self-criticology.** Cosmoethic criticism *predisposing* intellectual heterocriticophilia.

8. **Theoricology.** Proevolutionary verbaction *predisposing* cosmoethical irresistibility.

9. **Transparentiology.** Cosmoethic authenticity *predisposing* a strong presence.

Mediocritization. In the 21ˢᵗ century, unhinged Societies excel at valuing mediocrity and futility, *levelling down* their components. It is the squandering of the ideational potential of so many talented and polymathic consciousnesses that, envisaging not feeling excluded, end up by doing *more of the same,* notably in relation to their own existential choices, the theme of our next chapter.

BY PAYING THE ONUS OF DIFFERENCE, A COSMOETHICAL CALCULATING CONSCIOUSNESS PRIORITIZES SELF-EVOLUTION AND INTERASSISTANTIALITY, IN DETRIMENT TO SOCIN'S APPLAUSE, RECOGNITION, AND LAURELS.

Self-questioning. Do you, reader, unhesitatingly pay the price of assuming your own evolutionary level, your new ideas, and the clarification task?

20. Priority Evolutionary Choices

Choice. The **quality of the choice** indicates
the degree of the conscin's intelligence.[27]

Definology. *Choice* is the positioning, preference, predilection, election, or option of a consciousness before two or more possibilities, considering personal decision-making criteria.

Choices. The term *choose,* from the Old English: *ceosan,* Proto-Germanic: *keus;* Old Frisian: *kiasa;* Old Saxon: *kiosan;* Dutch: *kiezen;* Old High German: *kiosan;* German: *kiesen;* Old Norse: *kjosa;* Gothic: *kiusan,* and from Middle English: *chuse (16c-18c)* means "to seek out; to select from two or more; to decide; to test; to taste; to try; to accept; and to approve" is, as we can see, a very old word.

Priority. Prioritization is the catchword that captures the essence of consciential antiwastage. To help us understand its importance, this term, although young, but already informal in the English language (20th century), comes from the Old French *priorité* (14th century), and this in

27 **Vieira,** Waldo; *Léxico de Ortopensatas* (**Lexicon of Orthopensatas**); Foz do Iguaçu, PR: *EDITARES;* 2014; p. 616.

turn originates from Medieval Latin *prioritatem* (nominative *prioritas)*, fact or condition of being *prior* as in "the first (before the second); former; elder; before". In a nutshell: priority is what comes or should come first. What comes *second* may not be prioritary.

Definology. *Priority* is the condition of identifying the most important reality to be placed and dealt with first, in any given evolutionary moment, for a conscin, *per se*, or for the groupkarma (See **Vieira**, Waldo; Org.; ***Prioridade* (Priority);** ***Encyclopaedia of Conscientiology;*** Foz do Iguaçu, PR: *EDITARES/CEAEC;* 8th Ed. Electronic; 2013; p. 8,847 to 8,850).

Synonyms: 1. Essential. 2. Megarelevance. 3. Pre-eminence; primacy.

Antonyms: 1. Irrelevance. 2. Secondary; superfluous. 3. Superficial.

Evolutivity. The *priority evolutionary choice* is the decision of a lucid consciousness faced with different existential options, considering the evolutionary criterion of interassistantial relevance and the amplitude of the effects deriving from the self-positioning.

Antagonismology. Self-priority is the antagonism of self-wastage.

Self-reflection. It is worth the reader reflecting on: what aspects do you consider relevant to your major consciential decisions? If your answer does not emerge easily, the following considerations may help your self-reflections.

Choiceology. The following are 9 self-considerations, or self-evaluations, recommended for judicious consciousnesses facing critical existential decisions:

1. **Self-realism.** *There is no point in fooling yourself.* The priority is singular, unique, and essential, that is, it is an exercise of antidiscernment

to list 10 existential priorities. A person who has a dozen priorities has none.

2. **Self-positioning.** *Don't kid yourself.* To do what is evolutionary prioritary you will need to give up on something, to say "no" to other possibilities. To know what you need to discard in this *Age of Abundance* is as important as to know what to choose. *Less can be more.*

3. **Self-confidence.** *You cannot please everyone.* Prior to making a priority choice, it is worth asking whether the option for a particular task is just to please your peers or meet the expectations of the evolutionary group. Sometimes, *to lose is to win.*

4. **Self-awareness.** *There is no point in forcing your own nature.* When choosing something as an evolutionary priority, it is vital that it has to do with your interests, what you like, and your temperament, hence the importance of self-research and self-awareness.

5. **Antinaivety.** *Do not even try to be a hero.* Faced with a critical existential decision evaluate the duration of the task, the investment in time, energy, personal resources, your intentionality, and whose demand it is. If you have started a project, finish it before starting a new one. *Incompletism generates intra and extraphysical melancholy* (melin and melex).

6. **Self-prudence.** *It is no good to decide things on the spur of the moment.* Avoid committing yourself immediately to something that seems, at a first glance, *a helper's invitation.* Consider it first and ask for a deadline to reply. Ask for an e-mail to be sent with more details about the proposal, for example, avoiding unthinking reaction.

7. **Self-availability.** *It is of no use to always be available for everything and everyone.* The condition of evolutionary availability is not the same as prodigality or absence of judgement before the number of options on offer. Notice the difference between *being busy* and *being productive. He who wants everything loses everything.*

8. Interassistantiality. *You cannot save the Universe.* Discernment as to the pertinence of where the consciousness can be more useful is a fundamental when the time comes for making priority choices. Currently, there is an abundance of *conscientiocentric institutions,* projects, book proposals, and courses, challenging interassistantial endeavours, requiring arms and mentalsomas so they can be materialized. But which of these better represents the core clause of your existential program?

9. Self-priority. It does not help *jumping from branch to branch.* It is intelligent to first check if the new "must-do" demand is within the focus of your personal evolutionary priority. If it is not convergent, pay the price of the *onus of no,* already explained in this book, and reflect deeply on what you would have to give up to take on the new task. It is worth avoiding the posture of *jumping* from one activity to the next, one relationship to another, and/or one institution to another.

Neopriority. It becomes evident that a consciousness does not have one only priority throughout one single lifetime (or even in multiple existences). New priorities arise insofar as steps or stages are conquered in the evolutionary scale. It is worth emphasizing that an intelligent evolutionary choice will consider the context (and paracontext), scenario, and existential roles played at the time of the decision.

Criteria. The construction of rational criteria before making priority choices is one of the strategies used by a lucid antisquandering consciousness. Establishing principles for making fundamental distinctions, and standards for confronting, evaluating, and deciding before relevant existential realities is essential, to avoid running the risk of changing the fundamental for the secondary. Without criteria for making choices it becomes easier to make mistakes, and more difficult to get things right.

Evolution. From the standpoint of *conscientiology,* the *evolutionary criterion* is more advanced in relation to other intraphysical parameters for considering, for example, the following 9 pre-decision-making criteriologic qualifications, which we list here in alphabetical order, as self-assessing questions:

1. **Cosmoethicity:** Does the criterion consider cosmoethics, or just the normal moral conventions of intraphysical society?

2. **Holomaturity:** Does the criterion consider integral consciential maturity, expressed by a healthy and discerning manifestation of all the consciousness' vehicles of manifestation: soma, energosoma, psychosoma, and mentalsoma?

3. **Interassistantiality:** Does the criterion consider the best possible for all involved, or will it favour only oneself and/or the closest group of people?

4. **Mentalsomaticity:** Does the criterion consider the importance of advanced cognition, and that of the clarification task permeating to the maximum one's priority choices?

5. **Multidimensionality:** Does the criterion consider the parafact that nothing is unidimensional, and that an ampler cosmovisiologic vision includes other extraphysical dimensions and consciousnesses?

6. **Multiexistentiality:** Does the criterion consider the consciousness' past lives, evaluating possible perfected and stagnant self-mimicry?

7. **Orthoconviviality:** Does the criterion consider respecting all consciential principles, or merely the *Homo sapiens ilucidus'* rights?

8. **Proexality:** Does the criterion consider coherence and convergence of options, having the self-proexis as its megafocus, or does it fall totally outside the axis of an already identified existential program?

9. **Rationality:** Does the criterion consider logical, rational, and technical aspects when evaluating the options under analysis?

Technology. Conscientiology presents innumerable helpful evolutionary techniques for examining a consciousness' priority choice. It is worth highlighting here 3 feasible and very practical technologies proposed by Waldo Vieira, and with proven results, also tested by this author. Here they are, listed in alphabetic order:

1. *Personal Priorities Manual* (PPM): the most personal technical tool, capable of guiding a conscin through choices, or for determining essential goals for one's integral holosomatic, lucid, and cosmoethic self-development, in an objective, planned, and organized manner, within the perspective of the consciential paradigm, thus contributing to the attainment of one's existential completism (**Vieira**, Waldo; *Dicionário de Argumentos da Conscienciologia* (**Dictionary of Conscientiology Arguments**); Foz do Iguaçu, PR: *EDITARES;* 2014; p. 930.

2. *The 1-more Year of Intraphysical Life Technique:* the set of procedures envisaging the maximum planning of one's proevolutionary consciential efforts, from the supposition that the conscin only has 365 days left to live in the intraphysical dimension (**Rodrigues,** E.; *Técnica de mais 1 Ano de Vida Intrafísica* (**The 1-more Year of Intraphysical Life Technique**); *verbet;* In; **Vieira,** Waldo; Org.; *Encyclopaedia of Conscientiology;* Foz do Iguaçu, PR: *EDITARES/CEAEC;* 8th Ed. Electronic; 2013; p. 10,369 to 10,375).

3. *The 5-hour Self-reflection Technique*: the technique where a lucid conscin is willing to withdraw themselves into a quiet holothosene, disconnecting from the outer world, without carrying or making any notes, but only reflecting deeply upon the most relevant and prioritary themes of their present evolutionary moment and their existential recycling, for a full 5 consecutive hours (**Vieira,** Waldo; Org. *Autorreflexão de 5 Horas* (**5 Hours of Self-reflection**); *Encyclopaedia of Conscientiology;* Foz do Iguaçu, PR: *EDITARES / CEAEC;* 8th Ed. Electronic; 2013; p. 2,011 to 2,014).

Impact. The prospect of having only 1 more year of life in the intraphysical dimension, when considered seriously, has a striking effect on a lucid consciousness, who then has to choose what is prioritary and what can be accomplished in their short time left on this planet. It is important in this technique to ask yourself: what can I not miss doing in my present life – before my desoma, before *going belly up?*

Prophylaxis. The antiwasting consciousness makes a prophylaxis against limit-situations, such as the diagnosis of a terminal illness, maintaining existential commitments, not leaving gaps, or avoiding serious delays in evolutionary self-productivity.

Self-organization. Prioritization and personal organization go hand-in-hand. A consciousness with proevolutionary self-discipline sees the priority clearer, as they have already *spring-cleaned* their drawers, their personal agenda, and got rid of the superfluous from every-day life, whether objects or outdated ideas. Self-organization is in the antipode of self-wastage.

Challenge. Organizing one´s own life, and keeping it organized, is one of the greatest challenges as regards self-decision on consciential antiwastage. The first discipline is that of thoughts, feelings, and energies. However, an organized working station, good filing systems, and identifiable folders, updated diary, well-kept intellectual work routines, among other healthy habits, contribute greatly to orthothosenity (healthy thosenes).

Technique. By getting organized the consciousness already exercises prioritization, as they have to exclude excrescences, the superfluous, and thosenic and energetic knickknacks in their environment and intraconscientiality (See **Arakaki**, Kátia; *Antibagulhismo Energético* (**Antienergetic-Rubbish**); Foz do Iguaçu, PR: *EDITARES;* 2015; p. 33 to 47, and 123 to 140).

Coherence. *Self-organization is coherence between what you think, what you feel, and what you do* (**Vieira,** Waldo; *Dicionário de Argumentos da Conscienciologia* (Dictionary of Conscientiology Arguments); Foz do Iguaçu, PR: *EDITARES;* 2014; p. 313).

Minutiae. Self-discipline starts with the minutiae of everyday life. They count greatly on the accountancy of the *antiwastage-product* of a lifetime. A mere clock or watch, for example, not adjusted after *daylight saving time changes,* can mean lateness, and delay for important appointments.

Antiobsessiveness. Here we are not discussing obsessiveness with the organization of one's daily life as manifested by obsessive-compulsive disorder (OCD) patients. A lucid consciousness, meanwhile, does not suffer when a pen is out of its usual place, but simply puts it in the right place after use. An OCD sufferer is disturbed by the slightest changes in their routine of obsessive rituals. A self-organized intermissivist consciousness preventatively makes sure external and internal *chaos* do not severely disturb manifestation.

Self-motivation. The increase of proevolutionary productivity resulting from self-organization is going to motivate the consciousness who, upon seeing the results of their discipline, will seek to maintain their homeostatic pattern in order to maintain the rhythm of their production.

Freedom. The author Waldo Vieira argued in favour of self-organization by offering his own example, and affirming that meeting intraphysical needs with disciplined routines frees the person from human life enabling the individual to manifest themselves only as a "consciousness". Thus, paraperceptions, multidimensional interconsciential connections, and self-potentials are amplified.

Exemplarism. Vieira's intellectual productivity is well-known: he wrote dozens of books, among which 4 technical treatises, 3 dictionaries (all with well over 900 pages), and organized the proposed neoscience open *Encyclopaedia of Conscientiology,* leaving 2,019 entries or verbets of his own authorship. Each verbet is on average 5 pages long. In July 2015, the *Encyclopaedia of Conscientiology* registered an historical mark: 500 co-authors, in addition to its proposer, with about 4 thousand verbets.

Technicality. When questioned on various occasions about his self-organization techniques, in view of his extensive intellectual productivity, the versatile researcher used to say he just used one technique: *the disorganize while organizing technique.*

Antidispersiveness. Overcoming recurrent indiscipline, by organizing to the maximum every area of life, is a prophylaxis to consciential dispersiveness, *the villain* when a consciousness seeks antiwastage. It is highly relevant that we live lucidly with self-organization in this *Age of Abundance* of all sorts of rubbish and distractions.

Sense. Improving on our evolutionary choices and developing our sense of what is prioritary are conquests of a self-determined consciousness persisting in the megafocus of their self-proexis. It is always intelligent, from the perspective of evolutiology, to assess whether there are still dormant capacities and not yet applied potentials.

Adaptation. *Evolutionary intelligence* is the capacity to apprehend, learn, or understand and adapt to human life, based on the self-conscious personal application and theorical expansion of the already assimilated mechanism of personal, consciential evolution. This includes cosmoethicology, seriexology, and proexology, which defines the consciousness' self-discernment regarding rational consciential evolution, and lucid self-evolution in the dynamization of one's own self-thosenic and cosmoethic performance (See **Waldo**, Vieira; Org.; *Inteligência Evolutiva* (**Evolutionary Intelligence**); *Encyclopaedia of Conscientiology;* Foz do Iguaçu, PR: *EDITARES/CEAEC;* 8th Ed. Electronic; 2013; p. 6,108 to 6,113).

Measure. The *evolutionary quotient* (EQ) is a hypothetical measure of the level of advanced existential intelligence developed by an intermissivist conscin until now, and can be assessed through the consciousness' theoricity in relation to self-priorities, their daily experience and use of the consciential paradigm and the principle of disbelief (See **Manfroi**, Eliana; *Quociente Evolutivo* (**Evolutionary Quotient**); *verbet;* In: **Vieira**, Waldo; Org.; *Encyclopaedia of Conscientiology;* defended at the *CEAEC Tertuliarium*, Foz do Iguaçu, PR, on: 18.08.2014).

Legacy. Success, even if only partial, before the demands of one's self-proexis, which returns evolutionary profit and composes the consciousness' existential patrimony, constituting their own evolutionary legacy, a theme we will develop in the next chapter.

IN CRITICAL PRIORITY DECISIONS, HE WHO USES PRE-DECISION CRITERIA AND TAKES INTO CONSIDERATION EVOLUTIONARY INTELLIGENCE (EI), COSMOETHICS, AND LUCID INTERASSISTANCE, GETS IT RIGHT MORE OFTEN

Self-questioning. Do you use rational criteria to make evolutionary decisions? Can you list right now the cosmoethical premises that map out your personal decisions?

21. Self-evolutionary Legacy

> **Graphothosene.** One's evolutionary legacy is mea-
> sured by the repercussion of one's clarification task.
> The greatest **graphothosenic honesty** is of the author
> conscin who writes about what they have experienced.[28]

Definition. *Evolutionary legacy* is the patrimony of achievements
a consciousness passes on to themselves (self-legacy) and their co-passengers (heterolegacy), in future resomas, notably those coming from
mentalsomatic and interassistantial labour, as in a *corpus* of advanced evolutionary ideas, published in clarifying books.

Synonyms: 1. Evolutionary heritage. 2. Cosmoethical legacy.
3. Evolutionary testament.

Antonyms: 1. Antievolutionary legacy. 2. Groupkarmic interprison.

Typology. A consciousness can leave different types of evolutionary inheritance to itself and other legatees, such as these 10, listed in
alphabetic order:

01. **Conscientiographic legacy.** Is the full body of a consciousness' written work, whether books, chapters in anthologies, articles,

---

28 **Vieira,** Waldo; *Léxico de Ortopensatas* **(Lexicon of Orthopensatas);** Foz do
Iguaçu, PR: *EDITARES;* 2014; p. 764.

courses, encyclopaedic entries or verbets, and other clarifying publications.

02. **Cosmoethical patronage legacy.** The donations and sponsorships to interassistantial evolutionary enterprises made throughout a consciousness' existence.

03. **Exemplary legacy.** The benign examples left with a sound intentionality and cosmoethical good attitude throughout a consciousness' existence.

04. **Fraternal legacy.** All the fraternal actions of theorical universalism carried out during a consciousness' existence.

05. **Intellectual legacy.** The libertarian ideas and intellectual production brought to the public throughout a consciousness' existence.

06. **Interassistantial legacy.** Is the sum of a consciousness' interassistantial actions of all types over their existence.

07. **Leadership legacy.** The set of assistantial leadership roles performed over a consciousness' existence.

08. **Self-relay legacy.** The full extent of a consciousness' evolutionary achievements, to be resumed and updated in a future existence.

09. **Teaching legacy.** The accumulation of work in the teaching of libertarian clarification, notably through volunteer work.

10. **Volunteer legacy.** The lucid volunteering performed in support of the clarification task.

Self-relay. The evolutionary logic of self-relay indicates the importance of preparing ourselves for our next existence through the undertakings initiated in our current resoma. In a future life these will be resumed, updated, and expanded.

Synthesis. Consciential antiwastage principally happens when there is lucidity about the fact that the non-use of evolutionary contributions and opportunities can also signify a waste of subsequent existences, considering the gap in the multiexistential self-relay of the self-squandering consciousness.

Analogy. It is worth comparing this with a simple relay race, when a member of the same team passes the baton to the next member to proceed towards the finishing line. A consciousness passes the *baton* of their own evolutionary legacy to themselves. What if there is nothing evolutionarily relevant to bequeath to yourself? *Self-wastage is self-sabotage.*

Self-reflection. The invitation we leave here, at this moment, is for the reader to deepen their self-reflection on the evolutionary legacy accumulated so far in current resoma. It seems obvious that the condition of consciential antiwastage is essential to the quality of this accumulated existential patrimony. The relation is simple: the less self-wastage the greater the productivity and the cosmoethical accumulation of *evolutionary assets.*

Self-assessment. It is better to measure results than to quantify tasks performed. In order to contribute to the suggested personal reflection, here are, as examples, in alphabetic order, 9 self-questions pertinent to the evaluation of one's own legacy, made through an objective measurement of the results already obtained:

1. **Applied megastrongtrait.** What are your *objective* contributions in the application of your already identified megastrongtrait and interassistantial mega-attribute?

2. **Change of paradigm.** What are your *objective* contributions to the change of the current intraphysical restrictive paradigm by comparison to the cosmovisiological consciential paradigm?

3. **Conscientiological teaching.** What are your *objective* contributions to emancipating claritask teaching activity in courses, lectures, debates, and events in institutions focused on consciential evolution?

4. **Cosmoethical criticism.** What are your *objective* contributions to the dissemination and experience of the *principle of disbelief,* that is, to cosmoethical criticism before any relative truth?

5. **Planetary holothosene.** What are your *objective* contributions to the improvement of the planetary holothosene, by means of qualifying your own thoughts, feelings, and energies?

6. **Fraternal recomposition.** What are your *objective* contributions to liberation from groupkarmic interprisons and fraternal recomposition before, sometimes centuries-old, ex-creditors?

7. **Healthy conviviality.** What are your *objective* contributions to the improvement of conviviality among all consciential principles, including phyto and zoo conviviality?

8. **Lucid volunteering.** What are your *objective* contributions when it comes to volunteer work and the consciential connection with non-profit proevolutionary institutions?

9. **Self-recycling.** What are your *objective* self-contributions before necessary effective intraconsciential self-recyclings?

Self-heritage. It is important to emphasize it is the intraconsciential patrimony expressed in self-improvement, self-polishing, applied self-strongtraits, self-coherence, and self-discernment, among others, that is the most relevant evolutionary legacy a consciousness can leave to themselves, as a self-legatee. It is equally worth adding that, if all these recyclings have been registered and published in the form of a clarifying interassistantial book, this self-inheritance will have even greater value. *Personal book: self-legacy.*

ACCUMULATING MATERIAL ASSETS IS STILL A PRIORITY FOR AN IMPORTANT PERCENTAGE OF HUMANITY. ACCUMULATING EVOLUTIONARY ASSETS IS A PRIORITY TO INTERMISSIVISTS LUCID REGARDING THEIR SELF-RELAY LEGACY.

Self-questioning. I would like to ask permission, at this final stage of the author-reader dialogue, to put to you the following critical question proposed in this book: if you desomated ***today,*** what is the quality or substance of your evolutionary legacy to yourself? Would you consider, as of ***today,*** that you made the maximum possible investment to acquire useful consciential assets for yourself?

Closing Arguments

Evolutiology. If **evolution** was easy, humanity would already have been better for millennia.[29]

Fact. In this *Age of Abundance,* which started at the end of the 20th century and perhaps will continue to last for hundreds of years, we can observe a striking reality: there are more opportunities, projects, and ideas to be implemented than we can accomplish in our current existence. There are more books to read than we will ever have the time for. There are more innovative and evolutionary projects than we will be able to embrace. There are more people to encounter than we will be able to interact with. There is more demand for assistance than what can be fulfilled by consciousnesses focussed on the evolution of all.

Evolution. Life asks a lot of every evolving individual, and sometimes we bury ourselves in everything new, without selectivity and discernment. The tendency for the inhabitants of Abundanceland is to become hoarders of useless experiences and *piles* of all sorts of useless rubbish. *Avoid hoarding worthlessness.*

---

29 **Vieira,** Waldo; *Léxico de Ortopensatas* (**Lexicon of Orthopensatas**); Foz do Iguaçu, PR: *EDITARES;* 2014; p. 659.

Essence. It is no longer a question of continuing to lead difficult, suffering lives in this 21ˢᵗ century, but rather leading wasted lives in the midst of all this abundance, due to an inability to prioritize the essential. A wasted existence can be compared to a photo that tries to encompass the whole landscape, the city, houses, people, and even objects, without losing anything, but does not focus on nor value the essential detail of the recorded scene, which would make the photo worthwhile. *Megafocus is megaintelligence.*

Sense. Every consciousness is an important minicog in the evolutionary maximechanism. Your life, dear reader, and also this author's, are essential and unique. Finding such uniqueness is the sense of existence itself, and a main antiwastage strategy. *All lives matter.*

Daily. Existential completism, as a trophy for consciential antiwastage, does not depend just on the success of a single proevolutionary project undertaken throughout a lifetime. It happens daily, when one actually experiences the *evolutionary useful day technique,* as presented in chapter 16. This strategy of making each day count and express *zero consciential waste* lies the application of the sense of evolutionary usefulness embedded in each intermissivist. To briefly revisit this technique, it is about cooperating, learning, and producing something of evolutionary value every day, in an individual and group way. *Be evolutionarily useful.*

Reciprocation. Another approach to antiwastage can be observed in the process of reciprocating what you have received, borrowed, and were assigned, in terms of existential contributions. Every investment, especially evolutionary assets, should generate dividends and profits to be shared. *To reciprocate is to give back.*

Self-reflection. Spending 5 hours deeply reflecting on a theme relevant to one's evolution is not wasting time, but rather investing in a fundamental technique to guide one's own existential program. Any form of consciential self-reflection, self-assessment, and self-audit, at any age, generates information and data that will support prioritary evolutionary choices. *Antiselfwastage is self-prioritization.*

Appraisal. Just to think that one's current life (yours, mine, all of us) is so valued because it can yield more than our 15 prior existences, is impactful for any lucid consciousness. The evolutionary market requires sure, correct investments, without detour or waste of resources and attributes. To possess an idle or a dormant capacity in one's proexis is like throwing evolutionary assets out the window. We can compare it with the person who keeps their money under the mattress or at home in a safe for the entire duration of their existence, without considering the *depreciation of currency.* One could have used it in a cosmoethical investment rather than becoming an anti-assistantial miser. *Proexological idleness impoverishes.*

Warning. Among the objectives of this *intermissivist's survival handbook* is the one serving as a warning of the *surplus* of evolutionary resources in our current *Age of Acceleration of Personal History.* As a pro-evolutionary scolding, here is a warning or a well-intended and claritaskal cosmoethical *earful* for you. However, the first one to *make the hat fit* is the author herself. *The author is always the first to read the book.*

Paradox. Many were the consciousnesses observed by this author who were labelled "wasted" in different groups and contexts. However, they all had something in common: they were more intelligent than the average. Paradoxically, the most capable, qualified, competent, creative, polyvalent, tachypsychic, and *productive* (exactly as it is written, yes) were identified as self-squandering. They were reciprocating far less than they could to the world. What is the reason for this? How can we understand the *paradox of wasted intelligence?*

Hypothesis. The research and proposal of hypotheses to answer these questions would require a new book. Nevertheless, it is worth providing you, reader, with some considerations at the end of this text. As examples, here are 5 facts contributing to the understanding of the paradoxical condition of wastage of one's own intelligence:

1. **Fact:** too much ease is discouraging, because human nature *still* needs challenges to act (adrenaline).

2. **Fact:** many consciousnesses *still* present low intellectual self-esteem and insecurity regarding their own capacities, even when with a high level of intelligence.

3. **Fact:** a gifted consciousness can attend to many demands. However, due to an absence of evolutionary priorities, *still* gets dispersed in this *Age of Abundance* of stimuli and opportunities.

4. **Fact:** not every high intelligence quotient is accompanied by consciential maturity and lucidity regarding essential evolutionary choices.

5. **Fact:** the fact of performing well, with quality, almost everything in which one "puts time and energy" into, *still* can predispose a consciousness to remain in the comfort zone and not seek new proevolutionary skills.

Lucidity. Even so, the good news is that despite living in the midst of a generally disoriented and still pathological intraphysical society, we are still living in an *Age of Lucidity*. Never before in Human History have so many ideas, books, windows of opportunity, libertarian movements been available, and so much proevolutionary interactivity, so many intra and extraphysical helpers, and so much leading edge clarification been open to every lucid consciousness who is aware and shrewd regarding self-evolution.

Legaciology. We conclude this short handbook on consciential antiwastage by reiterating the idea expressed in the penultimate chapter – that of evolutionary self-legacy. As a legatee to herself, this author can only hope to have been able to contribute in some useful way with a legacy of ideas. It would be extremely helpful if the readers qualify this work with pertinent suggestions, criticisms, and revisions. No heterocriticism will be wasted.

Invitation. Finally, borrowing one last orthopensata from Waldo Vieira, here is an unmissable invitation:

"**Bibliothecology.** We urge all young intermissivists and existential inverters, young men and young women, to start their transcendent research now, so that they can take advantage of the extraordinary opportunities for study and research that Earth is offering today, something never seen before. Thus, tomorrow, in their chronological third age, lucid, beyond the biological age of 65 they will become wells of advanced megaknowledge, sources of multidimensional wisdom, and **walking human *bibliothecas,*** dedicated to fulltime cosmoethical claritaskology".[30]

---

30 **Vieira,** Waldo; ***Léxico de Ortopensatas*** (**Lexicon of Orthopensatas**)**;** Foz do Iguaçu, PR: *EDITARES;* 2014; p. 286.

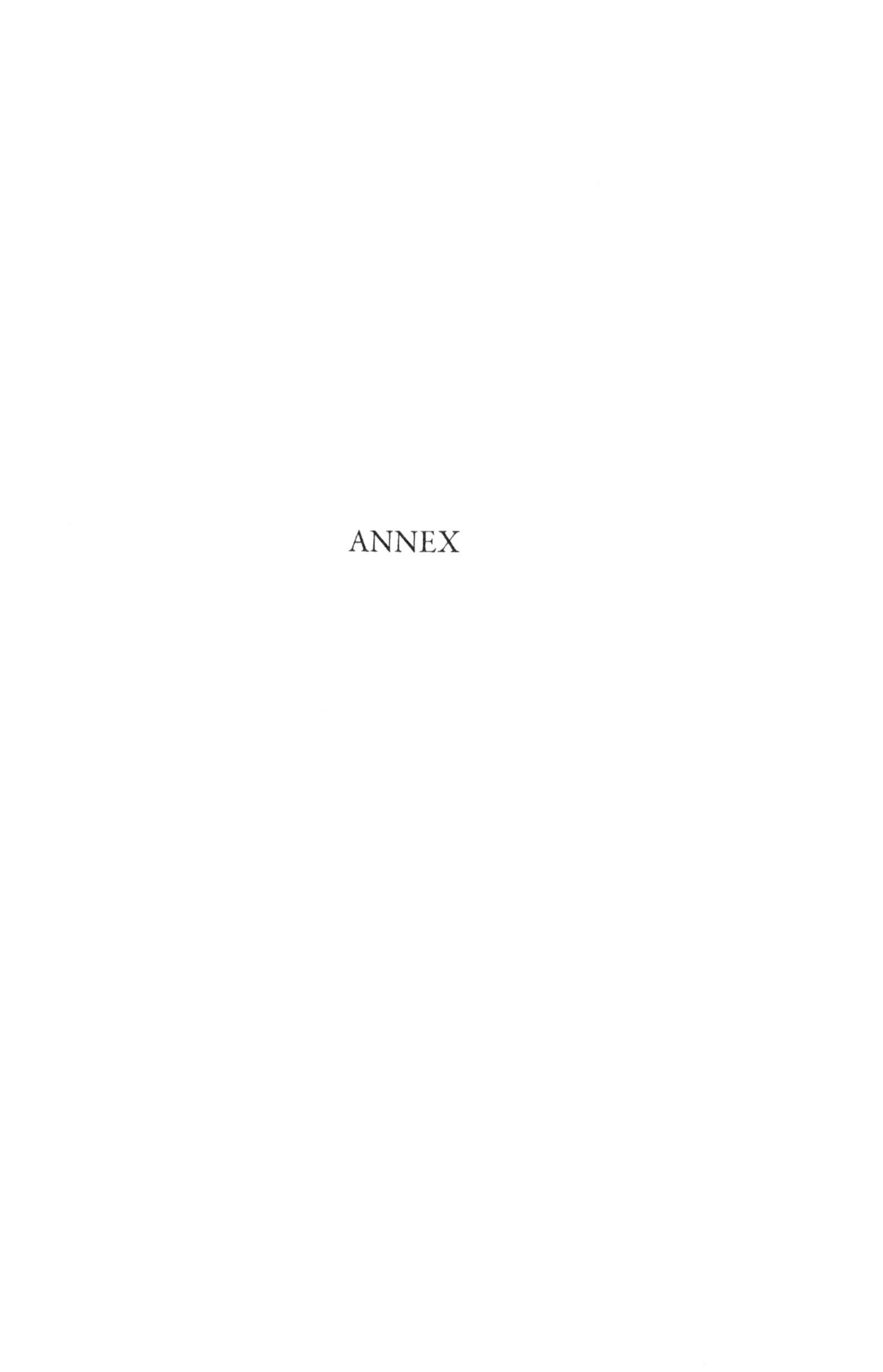

ANNEX

AVOIDANCE OF SELF-WASTAGE
(*SELF-PROEXOLOGY*)

I. Conformatics

Definology. *Avoidance of self-wastage* is the technique or set of attitudes, postures, behaviours, choices, prioritizations, decisions, intentions, and procedures adopted by the lucid intermissivist conscin avoiding wasting opportunities, strongtraits, capability, intelligences, geniality, innate ideas, paraprovenance, relationships, destiny reunions, and existential inputs, catalysts of the consecution of one's personal proexis and of existential completism.

Thematology. Homeostatic central theme.

Etymology. The term *avoidance* (avoid+-ance) first appeared in 14th century Middle-English, meaning "keeping away from, not doing something, or preventing something from happening". The term *self* comes from Old English, and previously from the Dutch *zelf* and the German *selbe*, initially used emphatically expressing the sense of "(I) myself". It can be used as noun, pronoun, adjective, and since the 19th century, as a verb. The term *wastage* (waste+age), (noun) is a derivative of the word *waste* (verb, noun, and adjective), which first appeared in 12th century Middle-English as *wast*, meaning "to consume, spend, use to no avail or profit, squander, fail or neglect to use, destroy, wear away, wear down, reduce in bodily substance, health or strength, enfeeble, destroy, devastate, ruin" (when used as a verb); "neglect, useless comsumption or expenditure, gradual destruction" (when used as a noun); "wild, desolate, barren, uninhabited, desert, left over, superfluous, rejected as useless or worthless, refuse" (when used as an adjective).

Synonymology: 1. Evolutionary self-wastage. 2. Prophylaxis of self-squandering. 3. *Time limit* proexis. 4. Application of evolutionary talents. 5. Investment in intraconsciential resources. 6. Cosmoethical pay-back of existential contributions. 7. Avoidance of self-sabotage; prevention of self-deceit. 8. Self-deintrusion.

Neology. The following 3 composed expressions: *avoidance of self-wastage, miniavoidance of self-wastage,* and *maxiavoidance of self-wastage* constitute technical neologisms of self-proexology.

Antonymology: 1. Waste of strongtraits. 2. Consciential ectopy. 3. Weaktraitist self-avarice. 4. Evolutionary pusillanimity. 5. Existential self-boycott. 6. Crass self-deception. 7. Self-intrusion.

Loanwordology: the *self-deception* of the self-help industry; *existentiale vacuum;* a *desviarium* of the pathological Socin; the *proexarium;* the *volontà ferrea.*

Attributology: predominance of mental faculties, notably that of self-discernment in relation to self-prioriology.

Megathosenology. Here are 3 trivocabular megathosenes synthesizing the theme: – *Autocide: fatal self-deceit. Let's sabotage self-sabotage. Self-wastage: anticosmoethical self-destruction.*

Colloquiology. Here are 7 common expressions related to the theme: the act of *scoring an own goal; missing the train of History; pulling the rug from under one's feet; tripping over one's own feet; shooting yourself in the foot; going yellow* in the face of any challenge; *finding the thread;* acting *without thinking; hitting the bull's eyes.*

Citatiology: – *The most intimate, deceptive, and at the same time the most defining relationship a human being has, is the one he has with himself* (Eduardo Giannetti, 1957–).

II. Factums

Thosenology: the personal holothosene of the good use of evolutionary opportunities; the prioriothosenes; the prioriothosenity; the lucidothosenes; the lucidothosenity.

Factology: the *Age of Abundance* of evolutionary inputs; the current resoma being worth 15 retrolives; the responsibility of having done an *Intermissive Course* (IC); the *volitioline* applied to one's self-proexis; *shamelessness*; cognitive dissonance; the low *evolutionary intelligence* (EI) quotient of the self-squanderer; the self-fiction; the self-intrusion; the traps; the ectopic gescons; the indoctrinations; the mysticisms; the self-sanctification; the pre-defeat; the minidissidence; the self-research data forgotten in a drawer; the banalizations; the valuation of the secondary and the depreciation of the priority; the deficitary omission; the anxiety caused by dormant talents; the reeducation based on evolutionary values; the task retaker; the overcoming of the consciential basement; the avoidance of setbacks; the consciential diversity providing the opportunities for new learnings; the growth crisis; the surplus omission; the avoidable self-mimesis; the avoidable neomimesis; the *foolishionary;* the sectarianism; the *market value* of the personal evolutionary file (PEF); the self-organization; the meaning of life; the *Personal Priorities Handbook* (PPH); the lucid projectability; the self-conscientiometry; the self-conscientiotherapy; the interassistantiality as maximum evolutionary anti-self-wastage.

Parafactology: the self-experience of the prophylactic vibrational state (VS); the recognition of the role-based assistance; the personal parapsychic signals indicating self-wastage; the intraphysical seedling generating an intermissive harvest of interassistantial fruits.

III. Detailing

Synergismology: the *synergism evolutionary unwasting–evolutionary orientor;* the *synergism routine-task-project-proexis.*

Principiology: the *principle of personal exemplarism* (PPE); the *principle of personal positioning;* the *principle of compulsory priority.*

Codiology: the *personal code of cosmoethics* (PCC) based on evolutionary values.

Theoriology: the *psychological theory of low self-esteem generating self-sabotage;* the *conscientiological theory of low self-esteem generated from self-corruption and existential self-indulgence;* the *theory of exemplary resilience.*

Technology: the *evolutionary useful day technique;* the *evolutionary prioritization technique;* the *only 1 more year of intraphysical life technique;* a *self-motivation-work-leisure trinomial technique;* the *technique of postponing immediate gains in favour of evolutionary profits.*

Voluntariology: the *international cosmoethical conscientiological volunteering.*

Laboratoriology: the *conscientiological laboratory of proexology;* the *conscientiological laboratory of paragenetics;* the *conscientiological laboratory of self-organization;* the *conscientiological laboratory of self-conscientiometrology;* the *conscientiological laboratory of thosenology;* the *conscientiological laboratory of evolutiology;* the *conscientiological laboratory of retrocognitions.*

Effectology: the *wasteful effect of electronotic science;* the *self-wastage effect of the materialist scientist;* the *disastrous effect of chronic procrastination;* the *potentiating effect of self-incorruptibility.*

Cyclology: the *cycle complexis-euphorin-euphorex.*

Enumerology: the qualified *Intermissive Course* (IC); the valued existential inputs; the applied personal strongtraits; the eradicated stagnant weaktraits; the prioritized evolutionary positioning; the accomplished life project; the celebrated existential completism.

Binomiology: the *binomial will-intentionality;* the *binomial reflection-decision;* the *binomial selectivity-evolution.*

Interactiology: the *interaction biological imperatives–environmental imperatives–evolutionary imperatives.*

Crescendology: the *crescendo map-analyse-illustrate-discuss-conclude;* the *crescendo who you are–who you can be.*

Trinomiology: the *trinomial power-status-prestige;* the *trinomial deviant sex-power-money;* the *trinomial pathological self-insincerity - self-corruption - self-sabotage;* the *trinomial self-discernment - self-organization - self-motivation.*

Polynomiology: the *polynomial reverie – self-deceit – hallucination - delirium;* the *polynomial self-wastage – incomplexis – melin – melex;* the *polynomial self-nonwastage – complexis - euphorin – euphorex.*

Antagonismology: the *antagonism minidissidence / maxidissidence;* the *antagonism false answers / real questions.*

Paradoxology: the *paradox of the highly capable intermissivist obtaining maximum success in their professional career, being a classic example of evolutionary self-wastage;* the *paradox of the engaged intermissivist who starts a master's degree and vanishes from the face of the earth;* the *paradox of the individual who receives a lot and contributes very little.*

Politicology: proexocracy; evolutiocracy.

Legislatiology: the *law of maximum evolutionary effort to take advantage of existential mishaps as opportunities for growth.*

Philiology: devianto*philia;* wasto*philia;* accidio*philia; procrastinophilia;* decido*philia;* neo*philia;* proexo*philia;* evolutio*philia.*

Phobiology: self-researchophobia; decidophobia; xenophobia.

Syndromology: the self-diagnosis and self-overcoming of the *proexical ectopy syndrome* (PES); the avoidance of the *Amiel syndrome;* the anti-example of the *Swedenborg syndrome;* the dribble in the *underestimation syndrome;* preservation of oneself from the *mediocrity syndrome;* dodge the *consciential dispersion syndrome;* elude the *deprioritization syndrome;* exempt oneself from the *wastage syndrome;* prevent the *paraphysiological abstinence syndrome;* guard oneself from *the savant syndrome.*

Manicology: risko*mania;* ludo*mania;* thanato*mania;* dipso*mania;* eroto*mania;* mystico*mania;* antico*mania;* megalo*mania.*

Mythology: the prophylaxis of *Ariadne's* thread in the labyrinth of the *Minotaur's* myth; the absence of caution in the *myth of Narcissus.*

Holothecology: the proexo*theca;* the weaktraito*theca;* the strongtraito*theca;* the recexotheca;* the invexo*theca;* the discernmento*theca;* the theorico*theca;* the convivio*theca;* the evolutio*theca.*

Interdisciplinology: proexology; prioriology; self-deceitology; deviantology; errology; decidology; profilology; discernmentology; strongtraitology; evolutiology.

IV. Profilology

Castology: the lucid intermissivist conscin; the lucid human bait; the strongtraitist conscin; the encyclopaedist conscin; the guinea-pig conscin.

Masculinology/Femininology: the self-wasted waster; the procrastinator; the spendthrift; the intermissivist; the existential invertor; the existential recycler; the self-decision-maker; the cognopolitan; the evolutionary co-passenger; the partner in an evolutionary duo; the evolutient; the exemplarist; the researcher; the tertulian; the verbetographer; the volunteer; the cosmoethical self-unwaster.

Hominology: the *Homo sapiens disperditius;* the *Homo sapiens incautus;* the *Homo sapiens acriticus;* the *Homo sapiens deviatus;* the *Homo sapiens autolucidus;* the *Homo sapiens vigilans;* the *Homo sapiens decidophilicus;* the *Homo sapiens neophilicus.*

V. Argumentology

Examplology: *mini*avoidance of self-wastage = the life-saving aid of a non-governmental organization (NGO) who values life, preventing the suicide of a depressed conscin; *maxi*avoidance of self-wastage = the helper assisting the intermissivist conscin at risk of imminent minidissidence.

Culturology: the *culture of megaprioritization;* the *culture of soft, light, and clean;* the *culture of superficiality in the Age of Void.*

Liberology. At no other time in Human History did freedom of consciential expression surpass the current level. An intermissivist publishes books and verpons with the certainty of not *ending up in a bonfire* together with the books. This fact alone represents a most unique evolutionary opportunity.

Taxology. According to *experimentology,* here are, in alphabetical order, 50 examples of evolutionary opportunities, often neglected, an aware intermissivist conscin can take advantage of within the conscin's present human existence:

01.   **Affective-sexual maturity.** To cultivate sex and affection with one's partner in an evolutionary duo.

02.   **Assistantiality.** To accept an *invitation from a helper.*

03.   **Bibliophilia.** To visit private and public bibliothecas.

04.   **Cinemascopic time-capsule.** To perform verbetographic defence.

05.   **Claritask.** To clarify, prioritarily.

06.   **Conscientiological itinerancy.** To travel guided by helpers.

07.   **Conscientiological teaching.** To avoid escaping the multidimensional classroom.

08.   **Conscientiological volunteer work.** To volunteer in a Conscientiocentric Institution (CI).

09.   **Contemporaneity.** To access the *science of sciences* simultaneously on the birth of the planet.

10.   **Council of the 500.** To regularly participate, centuries after the Greek-Athenian experience.

11.   **Daily *tertulias*.** To participate *in loco* or *online*.

12.   **Database.** To research in public, democratic, and free databases.

13.   **Deperticity.** To become completely and permanently deintruded in two decades.

14.   **Double degree.** To do a second degree, even in old age.

15.   **Evolutionary duo.** To build a harmonious partnership.

16.   **Existential savings.** To make a *nest egg.*

17.   **Favourable genetic heritage.** To maintain the good health received from one's parents.

18.   **Field courses.** To participate in field courses such as the *Acoplamentarium, Extension in Conscientiology and Projectiology 2* (ECP2), or *Advanced 2 (internationally), Projective Field,* and *Projectiotherapeutic Immersion.*

19.   **General Conscientiology Test.** To show up for the annual examination.

20.   **Guinea-pig conscin.** To *openheartedly* volunteer for the application of the conscientiometric technique.

21.   **Healthy retrocognitions.** To assemble your evolutionary *puzzle.*

22.   **Higher education degree.** To be in the 11% of Brazilians that have a degree (Base year: 2011).

23.   **Holocycle.** To do research in the megalaboratory of neoideas.

24.   **Holotheca.** To be a holotheca *mouse.*

25. **Intermissive course.** To honour the investment made by the evolutiologists.

26. **International travels.** To tour the world, overcoming inertia and laziness.

27. **Invexis.** To apply, when possible, the existential inversion technique.

28. **Multiple intelligences.** To employ modules developed in previous lives.

29. **Nutritional Intelligence.** To ban *silly* calories (starchy foods) and eat *intelligent* calories (fruit, vegetables, and proteins).

30. **Optimized childhood.** To live close to intellectualized adults during childhood.

31. **Paragenetics.** To use one's high abilities acquired in past lives.

32. **Penta.** To invest in interassistantiality for the rest of your life.

33. **Physical activity.** To guarantee useful longevity.

34. **Permanent-settling in a *Cognopolis*.** To move to a *city of knowledge.*

35. **Polyglotism.** To study languages since childhood.

36. **Productive longevity.** To avoid *hanging up the evolutionary trainers.*

37. **Proevolutionary technology.** To cure technophobia.

38. **Qualified education.** To access qualified schools in childhood and adolescence.

39. **Recexis.** To practice the existential recycling technique if necessary.

40. **Reconciliations.** *To sweat blood* to be *at peace with the Cosmos.*

41. **Self-learning.** To build up your own knowledge.

42. **Self-research laboratories.** To use these paratechnological parks.

43. **Self-researchophilia.** To notice, annotate, analyse, conclude, and publish.

44. **Smart detachments.** To give up on material and emotional *junk.*

45. **Sustainability.** To work *shoulder-in-parashoulder* with the helpers.

46. **Untransferable megastrongtrait.** To use one's major evolutionary talent in an interassistantial way.

47. **Verbetographic authorship.** To become a new verbetographer.

48. **Vibrational state.** To practice it 20 times a day.

49. **Writing strongtrait.** To avoid the existential *gaffe* of being able to write well from a tender age and not having published a book before age 49.

50. **Zooconviviality.** To care for pets (cats or dogs), during any phase of your life.

Avoidanceology. Under the optics of *Discernmentology*, the following are 5 postures to be avoided by intermissivists engaged in personal and group proexes:

01. **Avoid becoming a *vanishing act*:** members of the *invisible college* of volunteers.

02. **Avoid conscientiocentric autism:** the *oyster* effect of avoiding interaction.

03. **Avoid procrastination:** *pushing with your umbilicochakra* of your megadecisions.

04. **Avoid the consciential basement:** the opposition-antisocial behaviour.

05. **Avoid road detours:** intrusions caused by profligacy.

VI. Conclusion

Remissivology. By the criteria of *Mentalsomatology*, here are, for example, in alphabetic order, 15 entries from the *Encyclopaedia of Conscientiology*, and their respective specialities and central themes, evidencing a close relation to the avoidance of self-wastage, indicated for the expansion of more exhaustive, detailed approach by any interested researcher:

01. **Acceleration of personal history:** Evolutiology; Homeostatic.

02. **Antievolutionary dilettantism:** Antievolutiology; Nosographic.
03. **Consciential squandering:** Intraphysicology; Nosographic.
04. **Evolutionary choice:** Experimentology; Homeostatic.
05. **Existential savings:** Intraphysicology; Homeostatic.
06. *Five cycles:* Self-proexology; Homeostatic.
07. **Leverage of the proexis:** Proexology; Homeostatic.
08. **Gross evolutionary error:** Errorology; Nosographic.
09. **Mathematic life:** Holomaturology; Neutral.
10. **Lifelong establishment in a *Cognopolis*:** Resomatology; Homeostatic.
11. **Productive longevity:** Intraphysicology; Homeostatic.
12. **Sum of efforts:** Maxiproexology; Neutral.
13. **Task retaker:** Recexiology; Homeostatic.
14. *Underestimation Syndrome:* Parapathology; Nosographic.
15. **Wastage:** Ecology; Nosographic.

*A*VOIDANCE OF SELF-WASTAGE IS AN **URGENT** AND **UN-AVOIDABLE COMMITMENT** FOR ANY LUCID INTERMISSIVIST CONSCIN, VIA **COSMOETHICAL CONTRIBUTION,** ACHIEVED BY **GRAPHOCLARITASK, TEACHING, AND DAILY PENTA.**

Self-questioning. Have you, reader, been taking advantage of evolutionary opportunities in the realization of your proexis? Are you still a practitioner of *self-creepling*, promoting incomplexis, or are you already taking yourself seriously?

E. M. M.

BIBLIOGRAPHY

01. **Alvarenga;** Bianca; *A Angústia de Fazer Mais e Mais* (The Anxiety of Doing More and More); *Veja;* magazine; weekly; Ed. 2.476; Year 49; N. 18; 1 photo; 3 illus.; São Paulo, SP; 04.05.2016; pages 84 to 87.

02. **Arakaki,** Kátia; *Travões na Escrita* (Writing Blocks); article; *Scriptor;* magazine; annual; Year 5; N. 5; 1 email; 2 enus.; 1 microbiography; *União Internacional de Escritores da Conscienciologia* (UNIESCON); Foz do Iguaçu, PR; 2014; pages 29 and 30.

03. **Idem;** *Antibagulhismo Energético* (Energetic Rubbish): Manual; reviewers Erotides Louly; Flávio Buononato; & Sandra Tornieri; 238 p.; 23 chap.; 13 quotations; 1 curiosity; 24 emails; 52 enus.; 1 photo; 1 microbiography; 3 tables; 1 test; 21 websites; glos. 99 terms; 2 films; 110 refs.; alf.; 21 x 21 cm; br; *Associação Internacional Editares;* Foz do Iguaçu, PR; 2015; pages 41 to 84.

04. **Armstrong,** Thomas; *7 Tipos de Inteligência* (7 Kinds of Smart); transl. Oliveira Júnior; 368 p.; 15 chap.; 63 websites; 292 refs.; 21 x 14 cm; br.; *Record;* Rio de Janeiro, RJ; 2003; pages 39 to 57.

05. **Arnt,** Ricardo; *Sobre o Fim da Abundância* (On the End of Abundance); report; *Folha de São Paulo;* newspaper; daily; S/A; S/N; Section: *Opinião;* São Paulo, SP; 24.06.01; page A3.

06. **Ayan,** Steve; *Rir é o Melhor Remédio* (Laughing Matters); article; *Mente&Cérebro;* magazine; monthly; Year XVI; N. 198; 13 photos; 1 illus.; São Paulo, SP: Editora Segmento; July, 2009; cover and pages 36 to 43.

07. **Báez,** Fernando; *História Universal da Destruição dos Livros: Das Tábuas Sumérias à Guerra do Iraque* (*Historia Universal de la Destrucción de los Libros*); reviewers Gratia Domingues; & Raquel Correa; transl. Léo Schlafman; 438 p.; 35 chap.; 1 enu.; 1 microbiography; 1 website; 557 notes; 744 refs.; ono.; 23 x 16 cm; br.; *Ediouro;* Rio de Janeiro, RJ; 2006; pages 19 to 21, 131 to 199, 241 to 151, and 264.

08. **Balona,** Málu; *Autocura através da Reconciliação: Um Estudo Prático sobre a Afetividade* (Self-healing through Reconciliation: a practical study on Affectivity); pres. Daniel Muniz; pref. Cristina Arakaki; pref.to 1st edition Marina Thomaz;

pref. to 2nd edition Daniel Muniz; reviewers Alexander Steiner; *et al.;* 354 p.; 2 sections; 11 chap.; 18 emails; 1 interview; 56 enus.; 2 scales; 3 schemes; 125 expressions and popular sayings; 1 photo; 10 graphs.; 6 illus.; 1 microbiography; 5 synoptic tables; 4 questionnaires; 2 tabs.; 17 techniques; 5 theories; 15 websites; posf.; glos. 86 terms; 25 infographies; 20 scenographies; 72 films; 324 refs.; 2 appends.; alf.; 21 x 14 cm; br.; 3rd Ed. rev. and augm.; *Associação Internacional Editares*; Foz do Iguaçu, PR; 2009; pages 143 and 242.

09. **Bauer**, Susan Wise; ***Como Educar sua Mente: O Guia para Ler e Entender os Grandes Autores*** (The Well-Educated Mind: A Guide to the Classical Education you Never Had); pref. Gabriel Perissé; reviewers Valentina Nunes; & Francisco José Couto; transl. Gabriele Greggersen; 528 p.; 2 sections; 9 chap.; 1 enu.; alf.; 25 x 18 x 3 cm; br.; *É Realizações Editora;* São Paulo, SP; 2015; pages 11 to 520.

10. **Bauman**, Zygmunt; ***Modernidade Líquida*** (Liquid Modernity); transl. Plínio Dentzein; 258 p.; 5 chap.; 1 email; 1 microbiography; 1 website; 124 refs.; alf.; 21 x 14 cm; br.; *Jorge Zahar Editor;* Rio de Janeiro, RJ; 2001; pages 64 to 149.

11. **Idem;** ***Vidas Desperdiçadas*** (Wasted Lives); transl. Carlos Alberto Medeiros; 170 p.; 4 chap.; 129 refs.; alf.; 21 x 14 cm; br.; *Jorge Zahar Editor;* Rio de Janeiro, RJ; 2005; pages 117 to 164.

12. **Idem;** ***Vida para Consumo: A Transformação de Pessoas em Mercadorias*** (Consuming Life); transl. Carlos Alberto Medeiros; 200 p.; 4 chap.; 106 refs.; alf; 21 x 14 cm; br; *Jorge Zahar Ed.;* Rio de Janeiro, RJ; 2008; pages 70 to 106.

13. **Belik**, Walter; ***O Desperdício de Alimentos no Brasil*** (Food wastage in Brazil); report; *Valor Econômico;* newspaper; daily; Ed. 2.122; Year 9; São Paulo, SP; 24-26.10.08; page A17.

14. **Branco**, Adriano; ***O Mundo dos Desperdícios*** (The World of Wastage); report; *O Estado de São Paulo;* newspaper; daily; Year 130; N. 42,097; annex: *Economy;* São Paulo, SP; 19.01.09; page B2.

15. **Burke,** Peter; ***Uma História Social do Conhecimento: De Gutenberg a Diderot*** (A Social History of Knowledge: From Gutenberg to Diderot); transl. Plínio Dentzien; 242 p.; 9 chap.; 13 illus.; 547 notes; 700 refs.; ono.; 23 x 16 cm; br.; *Jorge Zahar Editor;* Rio de Janeiro, RJ; 2003; pages 15 to 21 and 27 to 29.

16. **Ceotto**, Bárbara; ***Diário de Autocura: Da Doença à Saúde Consciencial*** (A Diary of Self-healing: from Disease to Consciential Health); pres. & post. Leonardo Rodrigues; pref. Felix Wong; & Mário Oliveira; 224 p.; 16 chap.; 46 abbrev.; 15 quotations; 1 chronology; 22 emails; 26 enus.; 22 loanwords; 2 illus.; 1 microbiography; 21 websites; glos. 22 medical terms; 31 films; 1 note; 73 refs.; 1 append.; alf. geo.; ono.; 23 x 16 cm; br.; *Associação Internacional Editares;* Foz do Iguaçu, PR; 2014; pages 81 to 115.

17. **Couto**, Cirleine; ***Inteligência Evolutiva Cotidiana*** (Daily Evolutionary Intelligence); pref. Cristiane Ferraro; reviewers Editares peer team of reviewer; 190 p.; 30 chap.; 22 emails; 41 enus.; 1 photo; 1 microbiography; 3 tables.; 20 websites; 8 infographics; 4 films; 129 refs.; alf.; 23x16 cm; br.; *Associação Internacional Editares;* Foz do Iguaçu, PR; 2014; pages 28 to 30.

18. **Daou**, Dulce; ***Vontade: Consciência Inteira*** (Will: Consciousness in its entirety); Editares peer team of reviewers; 288 p.; 6 sections; 44 chap.; 23 emails; 226 enus.; 1 photo; 1 microbiography; 1 selection of the Encyclopaedia of Conscientiology *verbets;* 3 tables.; 21 websites; glos. 140 terms; 1 note; 133 refs.; 17 webgraphy; 1 append.; alf.; ono.; 23 x 16 cm; br.; *Associação Internacional Editares;* Foz do Iguaçu, PR; 2014; pages 63 to 84.

19. **Diamandis**, Peter H.; & **Kotler**, Steven; ***Abundância: O Futuro é Melhor do que Você Imagina*** (Abundance: The Future is better than your think); reviewer Lizete Mercadante Machado; transl. Ivo Korytowski; 424 p.; 6 parts; 19 chap.; 13 quotations; 6 enus.; 2 photos; 63 graphs.; 3 illus.; 5 maps; 2 microbiographies; 12 tables; post.; 797 notes; 1 append.; alf.; 23 x 15,5 cm; br.; *HSM;* São Paulo, SP; 2012; pages 51 to 67.

20. **Dyer**, Wayne W.; ***Seus Pontos Fracos*** (Your Erroneous Zones); transl. Mary Deiró Cardoso; 208 p.; 12 chap.; 42 enus.; 2 graphs.; 2 tabs.; 21 x 14 cm; br.; 25th Ed.; *Nova Era;* Rio de Janeiro, RJ; 2002; pages 9 to 33.

21. **Eisler**, Riane; ***O Cálice e a Espada: Nossa História, nosso Futuro*** (The Chalice and the Blade: Our History, our Future); transl. Terezinha Santos; 340 p.; 13 chap.; 4 chronologies; 7 maps; 78 refs.; ono.; 20 x 14 cm; br.; *Imago;* Rio de Janeiro, RJ; 1989; pages 13 to 200.

22. **Fernandes;** Pedro; ***Síndrome do Hiperconsumismo*** (Syndrome of Hyperconsumerism); *verbet;* In: **Vieira;** Waldo; Org.; ***Encyclopaedia of Conscientiology;***

electronic; CD-ROM; 2.498 *verbets;* 11.034 p.; 234 specialities; glos. 2.498 entries (*verbets*); 192 microbiographies; 147 tables; 191 verbetographers; 8th Ed. Digital; version 8.00; *Associação Internacional Editares;* & *Associação do Centro de Altos Estudos da Conscienciologia* (CEAEC); Foz do Iguaçu, PR; 2013; pages 9.953 to 9.958.

23. **Fischer,** Steven Roger; ***História da Escrita*** (A History of Writing); transl. Mirna Pinsky; 296 p.; 8 chap.; 1 email; 176 illus.; 1 website; 198 refs.; alf.; 22,5 x 14,5 cm; br.; *Editora UNESP;* São Paulo, SP; 2009; pages 13 to 18, 41, 53, 209, 210, and 278.

24. **Idem;** ***História da Leitura*** (A History of Reading); transl. Claudia Freire; 384 p.; 7 chap.; 1 email; 1 enu.; 7 illus.; 2 websites; 485 notes; 227 refs.; 23 x 16 cm; br.; *Editora UNESP;* São Paulo, SP; 2006; pages 9, 206 to 315.

25. **Flusser,** Vilém; ***A Escrita: Há Futuro para a Escrita?*** (Writing: Is there a Future to it); reviewer Gustavo Bernardo; 252 p.; 21 chap.; 21 x 14 cm; br.; *Annablume;* São Paulo, SP; 2010; pages 18 to 246.

26. **Fonseca,** Djalma; ***Técnica do Autoinventariograma*** (Self-Inventoryogram Technique); verbet; In: **Vieira;** Waldo; ***Encyclopaedia of Conscientiology;*** electronic; CD-ROM; 2.498 *verbets;* 11.034 p.; 234 specialities; glos. 2.498 entries (*verbets*); 192 microbiographies; 147 tables; 191 verbetographers; 8th Ed. Digital; version 8.00; *Associação Internacional Editares;* & *Associação do Centro de Altos Estudos da Conscienciologia* (CEAEC); Foz do Iguaçu, PR; 2013; pages 10,380 to 10,387.

27. **Fortes,** Leandro; ***Um Monumento ao Desperdício*** (O Centro Cultural de Goiânia está abandonado) – [A Monument to Self-wastage (Goiania's Cultural Centre is in a state of abandonment)]; article; *Carta Capital;* magazine; weekly; Year XV; N. 583; Section: *Seu País;* 4 photos; São Paulo, SP; 17.02.10; pages 20 and 21.

28. **Frankl,** Viktor Emil; ***Em Busca de Sentido: Um Psicólogo no Campo de Concentração*** *(Trotzdem Ja Sum Leben Sagen);* pref. to the USA edition: Gordon W. Allport; reviewer Helga H. Reinhold; transl. Walter Schlupp; & Carlos Aveline; 184 p.; 3 chap.; 4 enus.; 1 photo; 1 microbiography; 2 websites; 31 notes; 91 refs.; 2 webgraphies; 21 x 14 cm; br.; 31st Ed. rev.; *Sinodal;* São Leopoldo, RS; & *Vozes;* Petrópolis, RJ; 2008; pages 13 to 116.

29. **Gardner,** Howard; ***Inteligência: Um Conceito reformulado*** (Intelligence Reframed); reviewers Fátima Fadel; *et al.;* transl. Adalgisa Campos da Silva; 348 p.;

12 chap.; 240 notes; 395 refs.; ono.; 20,5 x 13,5 cm; br.; *Objetiva;* Rio de Janeiro, RJ; 2001; pages 11 to 116.

30. **Giannetti,** Eduardo; *Auto-engano* (Self-deceit); reviewers Cecília Ramos; & Ana Paula Castellani; 270 p.; 7 chap.; 279 refs.; 21 x 14 cm; br.; 6ª Ed.; *Companhia das Letras;* São Paulo, SP; 1997; pages 70 to 116.

31. **Idem;** *O Valor de Amanhã: O Ensaio sobre a Natureza dos Juros* (The Value of Tomorrow: na essay on the narure of interest); reviewers Octacílio Nunes; & Carmen S. da Costa; 338 p.; 4 parts; 20 chap.; epil.; 33 notes; 236 refs.; ono.; 30 x 20 cm; br.; *Companhia das Letras;* São Paulo, SP; 2005; pages 11 to 13, 87, 90, 124, 125, 171 and 174.

32. **Goleman,** Daniel; *Foco: A Atenção e seu Papel Fundamental para o Sucesso* (Focus); reviewers Joana Milli; Raquel Correa; & Fernanda Hamann de Oliveira; transl. Cássia Zanon; 294 p.; 7 parte; 21 chap.; 1 email; 8 enus.; 2 photos; 1 illus.; 1 microbiography; 1 test; 12 websites; 232 refs.; 18 webgraphies; alf.; 23 x 16 cm; br.; *Objetiva;* Rio de Janeiro, RJ; 2014; pages 81, 107, 108, 204, 248, 253, 254, 270 and 275.

33. **Guzzi,** Flavia; *Mudar ou Mudar: Relatos de uma Reciclante Existencial* (To Change or To Change: Reports of na Existential Recycler); pref. Málu Balona; reviewers Ana Luiza Rezende; *et al.;* 226 p.; 14 chap.; 19 emails; 1 interview; 11 enus.; 1 photo; 1 microbiography; 6 techniques; 3 websites; glos. 300 terms; 20 refs.; alf.; 20,5 x 13,5 cm; br.; *International Institute of Projectiology and Conscientiology* (IIPC); Rio de Janeiro, RJ; 1998; pages 10 to 22.

34. **Guzzo,** J. R.; *Analfabetos Voluntários* (Voluntary Illiterate); *Veja;* São Paulo, SP; 11 June, 2014; p. 100 and 101.

35. **Halévy,** Marc; *A Era do Conhecimento: Princípio e Reflexões sobre a Revolução Noética no Século XXI (L'Âge de la Connaissance: Príncipes er Refléxions sur la Revolution Noétique au 21 ème Sciècle);* transl. Roberto Leal; 36 chap.; 348 p.; 1 email; 2 websites; glos. 123 terms; 97 refs.; ono.; 23 x 16 cm; br.; *Editora UNESP;* São Paulo, SP; 2010; pages 22, 23, 42, and 43.

36. **Haymann,** Maximiliano; *Síndrome do Ostracismo: Mecanismos e Autossuperação* (Ostracism Syndrome: Mechanisms and Self-recovery); pref. Waldo Vieira; reviewers Erotides Louly; Helena Araujo; & Julieta Mendonça; 218 p.; 5 sections;

24 chap.; 17 emails; 134 enus.; 2 flowcharts; 1 photo; 1 microbiography; 2 tables; 16 websites; glos. 152 terms; 5 films; 202 refs.; 2 append.; alf.; geo.; ono.; 23,5 x 16 cm; enc.; *Associação Internacional Editares;* Foz do Iguaçu, PR; 2011; pages 21 to 48.

37. **Harris,** Sam; ***Carta a uma Nação Cristã*** (Letter to a Christian Nation); pref. Richard Dawkins; reviewers Otacílio Nunes; & Ana Maria Barbosa; transl. Isa Mara Lando; 92 p.; 1 enu.; 31 notes; 10 refs.; 13, 5 x 21 cm; *Companhia das Letras;* São Paulo, SP; 2007; pages 9 to 86.

38. **Idem;** *A Morte da Fé: Religião, Terror e o Futuro da* **Razão** (The End of Faith: Religion, Terror, and the Future of Reason); reviewers Huendel Viana; & Marcia Marchiori; transl. Claudio Carina; & Isa Mara Lando; 388 p.; 7 chap.; 686 refs.; 21 x 14 cm; br.; *Companhia das Letras;* São Paulo, SP; 2009; pages 67 to 73, 90, 95, 160, 166, 174, 204, 259, 263, and 287.

39. **Johnson,** Steven; ***Como Chegamos até aqui: A História das Inovações que Fizeram a Vida Moderna Possível*** (How We Got to Now: Six Innovations that Made the Modern World); transl. Claudio Carina; 236 p.; 6 chap.1 email; 1 scheme; 60 photos; 14 illus.; 1 map; 1 microbiography; 1 table; 1 website; 125 refs.; ono.; 23 x 16 cm; br.; *Zahar;* Rio de Janeiro, RJ; 2015; pages 8 to 212.

40. **Kahneman,** Daniel; ***Thinking, Fast and Slow*** *(Rápido e Devagar: Duas Formas de Pensar);* reviewers Ana Kronemberger; & Fatima Fadel; transl. Cássio de Arantes Leite; 608 p.; 5 sections; 38 chas.; 4 illus.; 400 notes; 2 append.; alf.; 23 x 16 x 3 cm; br.; *Objetiva;* Rio de Janeiro, RJ; 2012; pages 9 to 24.

41. **Kaplan;** Harold I.; **Sadock;** Benjamin J.; & **Grebb;** Jack A.; ***Compêndio de Psiquiatria: Ciências do Comportamento e Psiquiatria Clínica*** (Kaplan and Sadock's Synopsis of Psychiatric; Behavioral Sciences and Clinical Psychiatric); transl. Dayse Batista; reviewer Alceu Filman; 1.170 p.; 52 chap.; 95 illus,; glos. 100 terms; 95 photos; 60 graphs.; 666 tables; 20 schemes; 125 formules; 1 map; 4 enus.; 2 flowcharts; 2.902 refs.; alf.; 28,5 x 21,5 x 6 cm; enc.; 7th Ed.; *Artmed;* Porto Alegre, RS; Brasil; 1997; pages 308 and 309.

42. **Kostman,** Ariel; ***"Não Adianta Chorar"*** (No Use Crying); interview: Andréa Salgado; *Veja;* magazine; weekly; Ed. 1.852; Year 37; N. 18; 1 photo; São Paulo, SP; 05.05.04; pages 13 to 17.

43. **Leite,** Hernande; *Inteligência Financeira Proexogênica* (Proexogenic Financial Intelligence); *verbet;* In: **Vieira; Waldo; Encyclopaedia of Conscientiology;** electronic; CD-ROM; 2.498 *verbets*; 11,034 p.; 234 specialities; glos. 2,498 entries *(verbets);* 192 microbiographies; 147 tables; 191 verbetographers; 8th Ed. Digital; version 8.00; *Associação Internacional Editares;* & *Associação do Centro de Altos Estudos da Conscienciologia* (CEAEC); Foz do Iguaçu, PR; 2013; pages 6,114 to 6,123.

44. **Leite,** Marcelo; *Grupo tenta Convencer Jovens a não Dirigir depois de Beber* (Group Tries to Convince Youths to Avoid Driving after Drinking); report; *Folha de S. Paulo;* newspaper; daily; S/A; S/N; section: *Trânsito;* annex: *Cotidiano;* 1 photo; São Paulo, SP; 15.05.99; page 4.

45. **Lilienfeld,** Scott O.; **Arkowitz,** H.; *A Vida em Desordem* (Life in Disarray); *Mente&Cérebro;* magazine; São Paulo, SP; 2014; p. 50 to 53.

46. **Lipovetsky,** Gilles; *A Era do Vazio: Ensaios sobre o Individualismo Contemporâneo (L'ère du Vide Essais sur l'Individualisme Contemporain);* transl. Therezinha M. Deutsch; 198 p.; 6 chap.; posf.; alf.; 22,5 x 15,5 cm; br.; *Manole;* Barueri, SP; 2005; pages 20 to 34.

47. **Loche,** Laênio; *Determinantes do Conteúdo da Proéxis: A Abordagem Sistêmica da Evolução* (Determinants of a Proexis Content: a Systemic Approach to Evolution); article; *V Balanço Existencial;* Foz do Iguaçu, PR; 18-21.02.07; *Conscientia;* magazine; quarter; Vol. 11; 1-S; Section: *Temas da Conscienciologia;* 1 email; 33 enus.; 1 scale; 1 illus.; 1 table; 16 refs.; Foz do Iguacu, PR; February, 2007; pages 3 to 17.

48. **Idem;** *Aporte Existencial* (Existential Contribution); *verbet;* In: **Vieira; Waldo; Encyclopaedia of Conscientiology;** electronic; CD-ROM; 2.498 *verbets;* 11.034 p.; 234 specialities; glos. 2.498 entries *(verbets);* 192 microbiographies; 147 tables; 191 verbetographers; 8th Ed. Digital; version 8.00; *Associação Internacional Editares;* & *Associação do Centro de Altos Estudos da Conscienciologia* (CEAEC); Foz do Iguaçu, PR; 2013; pages 847 to 845.

49. **Lutfi,** Lucy; *Voltei para Contar: Autobiografia de uma Experimentadora da Quase-Morte* (I Have Returned To Let You Know: Autobiography of a Near-Death Experience); pref. Hernande Leite; reviewers Ana Flávia Magalhães Pinto; *et al.;* 248 p.; 2 sections; 19 chap.; 18 personal notes; 22 chronologies; 29 emails; 39 enus.;

1 photo; 6 illus.; 1 microbiography; 6 tables; 10 websites; 40 musicographies; 51 films; 1 note; 178 refs.; 5 webgraphies; alf.; geo.; ono.; 21 x 14 cm; br.; *Associação Internacional Editares;* Foz do Iguaçu, PR; 2006; pages 45, 50, 56, and 61.

50. **Luz,** Marcelo da; ***Onde a Religião termina?*** (Where Does Religion End); pref. Waldo Vieira; reviewers Erotides Louly; Helena Araujo & Valana Ferreira; 486 p.; 5 sections; 17 chap.; 12 documentaries and miniseries; 17 emails; 39 enus.; 149 wordloans; 1 photo; 1 microbiography; 15 acronyms; 2 tables; 16 websites; 79 infographics; 22 films; 571 refs.; 2 append.; alf.; geo.; ono.; 23,5 x 16 x 3 cm; enc.; *Associação Internacional Editares;* Foz do Iguaçu, PR; 2011; pages 373 to 383.

51. **Machado;** Cesar; ***Antivitimização: Alicerce para a Autoevolução*** (Antivictimization: Foundation for Self-evolution); pref. Alexandre Zaslavsky; reviewer Ninarosa Manfroi; 66 abbreviations; 328 p.; 3 sections; 19 chap.; 25 emails; 50 wordloands; 1 photo; 1 minibiography; 5 tables; 22 websites; 215 refs.; alf.; geo.; ono.; glos. 153 terms; 23 x 16 cm; br; *Associação Internacional Editares;* Foz do Iguaçu, PR; 2016; pages 163 to 170, and 225 to 234.

52. **Mackenzie,** Alec; ***A Armadilha do Tempo: Como Implantar um Plano de Ação Individual e Coletivo para Melhor Aproveitamento do Tempo Disponível*** (*The Time Trap: The Classic Book on Time Management);* Makron Books; São Paulo, SP; 1991; pages 228 to 250.

53. **Manfroi,** Eliana; ***Autopesquisa e Profilaxia da Síndrome da Ectopia de Proéxis*** (Self-research and Prophylaxis of the Ectopic Proexis Syndrome); article; *IV Jornada de Autopesquisa Conscienciologica;* Florianópolis, SC; 21-23.04.06; *Journal of Conscientiology (JofC);* Journal; quarterly; Vol. 8; N. 31-S; 7 enus.; 19 refs.; *International Academy of Consciousness* (IAC); London; UK; April, 2006; pages 193 to 204.

54. **Idem;** ***Crescendo Verbetógrafo-Maxiproexista: Assumindo a Identidade Interassistencial*** (The Crescendo Verbetographer-Maxiproexist: Assuming one´s Interassistantial Identity); artcile; *II Congresso Internacional de Autopesquisologia;* 15--17.11.13; Foz do Iguaçu, PR; *Conscientia;* magazine; Special Ed.; Vol. 17; N. 2; Section: *Artigo Original;* 1 email; 14 enus.; 3 refs.; *Associação Internacional do Centro de Altos Estudos da Conscienciologia* (CEAEC); Foz do Iguaçu, PR; July-September, 2012; pages 180 to 188.

55. **Idem;** ***Empreendendo a Evolução Pessoal através da Planificação Evolutiva*** (Undertaking Personal Evolution through Evolutionary Planning); article; *II*

Jornada de Administração Conscienciológica; São Paulo, SP; 12-15.10.06; *Conscientia;* magazine; quarterly; Special Ed.; Vol. 10; N. 1; Section: *Temas da Conscienciologia;* 1 email; 12 enus.; 3 tables; 12 refs.; *Associação Internacional do Centro de Altos Estudos da Conscienciologia* (CEAEC); Foz do Iguaçu, PR; January-March, 2006; pages 12 to 20.

56. **Idem;** ***Resiliência Interassistencial: A Força do Exemplo*** (Interassistantial Resilience: the Strength of Example); article; *Journal of Conscientiology (JofC);* journal; quarterly; Vol. 9; N. 36; 1 email; 4 enus.; 23 refs.; *International Academy of Consciousness* (IAC); Evoramonte; Portugal; 2007; pages 427 to 435.

57. **Idem;** ***Autauditoria Quinquagenária; Binômio Resiliência-Exemplarismo; Desambição Carreirística; Evitação do Autodesperdício*** (Quinquagenarian Self-audit; Resilience-Exemplarism Bynomial; Career Non-ambition; Avoidance of Self-wastage); *verbets;* In: **Vieira;** Waldo; Org.; ***Encyclopaedia of Conscientiology;*** electronic; CD-ROM; 2.498 verbets; 11.034 p.; 234 specialities; glos. 2.498 entries (*verbets*); 192 microbiographies; 147 tables; 191 verbetographers; 8th Ed. Digital; version 8.00; *Associação Internacional Editares;* & *Associação do Centro de Altos Estudos da Conscienciologia* (CEAEC); Foz do Iguaçu, PR; 2013; pages 1,235 to 1,240, 2,462 to 2,466, 3,884 to 3,888, and 4,855 to 4,860.

58. **Martyn,** Lyons. ***Livro: Uma História Viva*** (Books, a Living History); reviewers Ana Beatriz Viana Souto Maior; Cleber Siqueira; Denise de Almeida & Maristela de Nóbrega; transl. Luís Carlos Borges; 224 p.; 5 chap.; 57 refs.; 220 illus.; ono.; 26 x 19,5 cm; enc.; *Editora Senac;* São Paulo, SP; 2011; page 11.

59. **Masi,** Domenico de; ***O Futuro chegou: Modelos de Vida para uma Sociedade Desorientada*** *(Il Futuro è arrivato);* transl. Marcelo Costa Sievers; 768 p.; 14 chap.; 382 refs.; ono.; 22 x 15 x 4,5 cm; br.; *Quintanda Cultural* & *Casa da Palavra;* Rio de Janeiro, RJ; 2014; pages 23 to 605.

60. **Idem;** ***O Ócio Criativo*** *(Ozio Creativo);* Interview: Maria Serena Palieri; reviewers Lucia Ribeiro de Souza; Luiz Cavalcanti; & Sergio Bellinelo Soares; transl. Lea Manzi; 336 p.; 14 chap.; 1 scheme; 5 illus.; 20 x 14 cm; br.; *Sextante;* Rio de Janeiro, RJ; 2000; pages 296 to 336.

61. **Melillo,** Aldo; & **Ojeda,** Elbio Néstor Suárez; ***Resiliência: Descobrindo as Próprias Fortalezas*** *(Resiliencia: Descubriendo las Proprias Fortalezas);* transl. Valério

Campos; 160 p.; 12 chap.; 163 refs.; 23 x 21 cm; br.; 2005; *Artmed;* Porto Alegre, RS; pages 15 to 38, and 59 to 72.

62. **Merril**, Roger; & **Merril**, Rececca; *Life Matters (Questões Fundamentais da Vida: Criando um Equilíbrio Dinâmico entre trabalho, família, tempo e dinheiro);* pref. Stephen Covey; reviewers Clara Diament; *et al.;* transl. Sonia Maria Moitrel Schwarts; 288 p.; 7 chap.; 34 quotations; 5 emails; 1 enu.; 3 schemes; 1 test; 5 websites; 85 notes; 40 refs.; 22,5 x 16 cm; br.; *Sextante;* Rio de Janeiro, *RJ; 2004;* pages 161, 214, 215, 229, and 257.

63. **Mota**, Tathiana; ***Curso Intermissivo: Você se Preparou para os Desafios da Vida Humana?*** (Intermissive Course: Have You Prepared for Human Life's Challenges); pres. Ana Luiza Rezende; reviewer Cesar Machado; reviewer Laura Bruna Araújo; 200 p.; 3 sections; 10 chap.; 2 emails; 10 questionnaires; 3 websites; posf.; 83 refs.; 14 webgraphies; 2 annexes; alf.; 23 x 16 cm; br.; *Editares;* Foz do Iguaçu, PR; 2016; pages 61 to 63.

64. **Musskopf**, Tony; ***Autenticidade Consciencial*** (Consciential Authenticity); pref. Kátia Arakaki; reviewers Claudio Lima; *et al.;* 376 p.; 107 chap.; 6 sections; 71 abbrev.; 22 emails; 155 enus.; 81 wordloans; 1 microbiography; 1 questi of consciential authenticity with 10 questions and 10 answers; 3 tables; 19 websites; glos. 237 terms; glos. 11 terms (specialized. neological); 6 films; 508 refs.; 1 annex; alf.; geo.; ono.; 23,5 x 16,5 cm; br.; *Associação Internacional Editares;* Foz do Iguaçu, PR; 2012; pages 212 to 215.

65. **Nonato**, Alexandre; *et al.; **Inversão Existencial: Autoconhecimento, Assistência e Evolução desde a Juventude*** (Existential Inversion: Self-awareness, Assistance, and Evolution since Youth); pref. Waldo Vieira; reviewers Helena Alves Araújo; & Erotides Louly; 304 p.; 70 chap.; 17 emails; 62 enus; 16 photos; 5 microbiographies; 7 tables; 17 websites; glos. 155 terms; 376 refs.; 1 append.; alf.; 23 x 16 cm; br.; *Associação Internacional Editares;* Foz do Iguaçu, PR; 2011; pages 22, 50, and 51.

66. **Oliveira**; Gesner; ***O Fim da Era do Desperdício*** (The End of the Age of Wastage); *Veja;* magazine; weekly; Ed. 2.385; Year 47; N. 32; 1 photo; *Editora Abril;* São Paulo, SP; 06.08.2014; pages 17 to 21.

67. **Ribeiro**, Fabiana; ***Desperdício, Não!*** (Brasileiro é o que mais se preocupa com Descarte de Alimentos, diz Estudo em 8 Países) [Waste Not! (Brazilians Worry the

Most about Food Disposal, says a study conducted in 8 countries)]; report; *O Globo;* newspaper; daily; Year LXXXVII; N. 28.556; annex: *Economia;* Rio de Janeiro, RJ; 12.11.11; page 31.

68. **Rodrigues;** Elisabeth; ***Técnica de Mais 1 Ano de Vida Intrafísica*** (The 1 Year Left of Intraphysical Life Technique); *verbet;* In: **Vieira;** Waldo; ***Encyclopaedia of Conscientiology;*** electronic; CD-ROM; 2.498 *verbets;* 11.034 p.; 234 specialities; glos. 2.498 entries *(verbets);* 192 microbiographies; 147 tables; 191 verbetographers; 8th Ed. Digital; version 8.00; *Associação Internacional Editares;* & *Associação do Centro de Altos Estudos da Conscienciologia* (CEAEC); Foz do Iguaçu, PR; 2013; pages 10.369 to 10.375.

69. **Rosa,** Diego; ***Diálogo sobre o Desperdício*** (A Dialogue on Wastage); report; *A Notícia;* newspaper; daily; N. 24.017; 1 photo; Section: *Cidade;* Joinville, SC; 11.01.07; page 8.

70. **Rossa,** Dayane; ***Trafor Ocioso*** (Stagnant Strongtrait); *verbet;* In: **Vieira;** Waldo; ***Encyclopaedia of Conscientiology;*** electronic; CD-ROM; 2.498 *verbets;* 11.034 p.; 234 specialities; glos. 2.498 entries *(verbets);* 192 microbiographies; 147 tables; 191 verbetographers; 8th Ed. Digital; version 8.00; *Associação Internacional Editares;* & *Associação do Centro de Altos Estudos da Conscienciologia* (CEAEC); Foz do Iguaçu, PR; 2013; pages 10,618 to 10,623.

71. **Idem;** ***Oportunidade de Viver: Estudo sobre a Existência Humana e o Sentido da Vida*** (Opportunity to Live: a Study on Human Existence and the Meaning of Life); pref. Amin Lascani; reviewers Editares peer reviewer team; 328 p.; 8 sections; 47 chap.; 22 emails; 192 enus.; 1 photo; 1 mini-cv; 2 tables; 20 websites; glos. 179 terms; 10 films; 199 refs.; alf.; 23 x 16 cm; br.; *Associação Internacional Editares;* Foz do Iguaçu, PR; 2014; pages 183 to 198.

72. **Rosenberg,** B. Marshall; ***Comunicação Não-Violenta: Técnicas para Aprimorar Relacionamentos Pessoais e Profissionais*** *(Nonviolent Communication: A Language of Life);* pref. Arun Gandhi; reviewer Dominic Barter; transl. Mário Vilela; 286 p.; 13 chap.; 6 depositions; 3 emails; 40 enus.; 1 table; 5 tests; 3 websites; 55 refs.; alf.; 21 x 14 cm; br.; 3ª Ed.; *Ágora;* São Paulo, SP; 2006; pages 37 to 253.

73. **Santarosa,** Daniela; ***Desperdício na Saúde*** (Hepatite B causa 25% dos Descartes de Córnea no RS) – [A Waste of Health (Hepatitis B causes 25% of cornea

discard in RS); report; *Zero Hora;* newspaper; daily; Year 49; N. 17,157; section: *Geral;* Porto Alegre, RS; 27.09.12; page 36.

74. **Schmit,** Luimara; ***Programa de Recéxis: Recurso Conscienciométrico para Autoplanejamento*** (Recexis Programming: a Conscientiometric resource for self-planning); article; *I Congresso Internacional de Autopesquisologia & V Jornada de Autopesquisa;* Rio de Janeiro, RJ; 13-15.11.10; *Conscientia;* magazine; quarterly; special ed.; Vol. 14; N. 1; section: *Temas da Conscienciologia;* 1 email; 10 enus.; 1 microbiography; 14 tables; 6 refs.; *Associação Internacional do Centro de Altos Estudos da Conscienciologia* (CEAEC); Foz do Iguaçu, PR; January-March, 2010; pages 25 to 38.

75. **Stamateas,** Bernardo; ***Autossabotagem: Reconheça e mude as Atitudes que você toma contra si mesmo (Autoboicot)*** – [Self-sabotage: Recognize it and change the attitude against yourself (self-boycott)]; transl. Sandra Martha Dolinsky; 190 p.; 14 chap.; 1 email; 74 enus.; 1 photo; 1 microbiography; 2 websites; 2 notes; 33 refs.; 21 x 14 cm; br.; *Academia de Inteligência;* São Paulo, SP; 2009; pages 65 to 84.

76. **Stédile,** Eliane; & **Facury,** Marco Antônio Rocha; ***Autovivenciograma: Técnica para Autopesquisa*** (Self-experencogram: Self-research technoque); article; *I Congresso Internacional de Autopesquisologia & V Jornada de Autopesquisa;* Rio de Janeiro, RJ; 13-15.11.10; *Conscientia;* magazine; quarterly; Special Ed.; Vol. 14; N. 1; Section: *Temas da Conscienciologia;* 2 emails; 12 enus.; 2 microbiographies; 1 technique; 2 notes; 10 refs.; 2 annexes; *Associação Internacional do Centro de Altos Estudos da Conscienciologia* (CEAEC); Foz do Iguaçu, PR; January-March, 2010; pages 100 to 109.

77. **Steel,** Piers; ***A Equação de Deixar para Depois: Livre-se das Tentações e faça o que tem que Ser feito agora*** (*The Procrastination Equation*); transl. Gabriel Zide Neto; 278 p.; 10 chap.; 1 email; 1 microbiography; 348 refs.; 23 x 16 cm; br.; *BestSeller;* Rio de Janeiro, RJ; 2012; pages 8 to 101.

78. **Strauch,** Barbara; ***O Melhor Cérebro da sua Vida: Segredos e Talentos da Maturidade*** (*The Secret Life of the Grown-up: The Surprising Talens of the Middle-aged Mind*); transl. Vera Ribeiro; 222 p.; 11 chap.; 1 microbiography; 23 x 16 cm; br.; *Zahar;* Rio de Janeiro, RJ; 2011; pages 23 to 213.

79. **Teles,** Mabel; ***Profilaxia das Manipulações Conscienciais*** (Prophylaxis of Consciential Manipluation); collaborators Eduardo Ferreira; & Ivo Valente; pref.

Flávia Guzzi; reviewers Ana Flávia Magalhães; *et al.;* 346 p.; 6 parts; 44 chap.; 1 chronology; 22 emails; 223 enus.; 1 photo; 1 microbiography; 32 questions; 2 tables; 10 websites; glos. 182 terms; 10 films; 344 refs.; 1 append.; alf.; 21 x 14 cm; br.; *Associação Internacional do Centro de Altos Estudos da Conscienciologia* (CEAEC); & *Associação Internacional Editares;* Foz do Iguaçu, PR; 2007; pages 32 to 79.

80. **Idem;** *Zéfiro: A Paraidentidade Intermissiva de Waldo Vieira* (Zephyr: The Intermissive Paraidentity of Waldo Vieira); reviewers Erotides Louly; *et. al.;* 240 p.; 3 sections; 14 chap.; 113 quotations; 22 emails; 32 enus.; 37 photos; 1 timeline; 1 microbiography; 2 tables; 20 websites; glos. 210 terms; 45 refs.; alf.; geo.; ono.; 23 x 16 cm; br.; *Associação Internacional Editares;* Foz do Iguaçu; PR; 2014; pages 131 to 141.

81. **Idem;** *Bônus do Não* (The Bonus of No); *verbet;* In: **Vieira;** Waldo; *Encyclopaedia of Conscientiologyy;* electronic; CD-ROM; 2.498 *verbets;* 11.034 p.; 234 specialities; glos. 2.498 entries (*verbets*); 192 microbiographies; 147 tables; 191 verbetographers; 8ª Ed. Digital; version 8.00; *Associação Internacional Editares;* & *Associação do Centro de Altos Estudos da Conscienciologia* (CEAEC); Foz do Iguaçu, PR; 2013; pages 2.535 to 2.539.

82. **Theodoro Filho,** Jaci Alvarenga; *A Cultura do Desperdício* (The Culture of Wastage); report; *Gazeta do Rio;* newspaper; daily; S/A; S/N; section: *Opinião;* Rio de Janeiro, RJ; 2001; 16.06.01; page 2.

83. **Toledo,** Flávio; *Desperdício de Talentos* (Waste of Talent); report; *Gazeta do Rio;* newspaper; daily; Year 2; N. 291; section: *Opinião;* Rio de Janeiro, RJ; 23.03.99; page 2.

84. **VandenBos,** Gary R.; Org.; *Dicionário de Psicologia da APA (APA Dictionary of Psychology);* reviewers Maria Lucia Tiellet Nunes; & Giana Bitencourt Frizzo; transl. Daniel Bueno; Maria Adriana Veríssimo Veronese; & Maria Cristina Monteiro; 1.040 p.; glos. 25.000 terms; 4 apend.; 28 x 21 cm; enc.; *Artmed;* Porto Alegre, RS; 2010; page 845.

85. **Veja;** *Ranking do Desperdício* (Wastage Ranking); Redação; magazine; weekly; Ed. 1.665; Year 33; N. 36; Section: *Para Usar;* 5 photos; 1 table; São Paulo, SP; 06.09.2000; page 150.

86. **Veja;** *A Angústia do Excesso de Informação* (Excess of Information Anxiety); Redação; magazine; Year 34; N. 35; Section: *Comportamento;* São Paulo, SP; 05.09.2001; pages 62 to 66.

87. **Vicenzi,** Luciano; *Coragem para Evoluir* (Courage to Evolve); pref. Málu Balona; reviewers Gisele Salles; Karina Thomaz; & Márcia Abrantes; 188 p.; 8 chap.; 21 emails; 1 interview; 51 enus.; 1 photo; 2 illus.; 1 microbiography; 2 tables; 3 websites; glos. 37 terms; 50 refs.; alf.; 21 x 14 cm; br.; *International Institute of Projectiology and Conscientiology* (IIPC); Rio de Janeiro, RJ; 2001; pages 17, 79, 86, 87, 149, and 151.

88. **Waldo;** Vieira; *100 Testes da Conscienciometria* (100 Tets of Conscientiometry); reviewer Alexander Steiner; 232 p.; 100 chap.; 15 emails; 103 enus.; 1 photo; 1 microbiography; 123 questions; 2 websites; 14 refs.; alf.; 21 x 14 cm; br.; *International Institute of Projectiology and Conscientiology* (IIPC); Rio de Janeiro, RJ; 1997; pages 150 to 153.

89. **Idem;** *200 Teáticas da Conscienciologia: Especialidades e Subcampos* (200 Theactics of Conscientiology: Specialities and Subfields); reviewers Alexander Steiner; *et al.;* 260 p.; 200 chap.; 15 emails; 8 enus.; 1 photo; 1 microbiography; 13 refs.; alf,; 21 x 14 cm; br.; *International Institute of Projectiology and Conscientiology* (IIPC); Rio de Janeiro, RJ; 1997; pages 22, 30, 40, 41, 43, 57, and 204.

90. **Idem;** *700 Experimentos da Conscienciologia* (700 Experiments of Conscientiology); 1.058 p.; 40 sections; 100 sub-sections; 700 chap.; 147 abbrev.; 1 chronology; 100 dates; 1 email; 600 enus.; 272 wordloans; 2 tables; 300 tests; glos. 280 termos; 5.116 refs.; alf.; geo.; ono.; 28,5 x 21,5 x 7 cm; enc.; *International Institute of Projectiology and Conscientiology* (IIPC); Rio de Janeiro; RJ; 1994; pages 565 to 570, 632, 633, and 682.

91. **Idem;** *Conscienciograma: Técnica de Avaliação da Consciência Integral* (Conscientiogram: Technique for Assessment of the Consciousness in its entirety); reviewer Alexander Steiner; 344 p.; 150 abbrev.; 106 subjects of evalutation; 3 emails; 11 enus.; 100 evaluation sheets; 1 photo; 1 microbiography; 100 qualities of the consciousness; 100 titles on evaluation sheets; 1 website; 2.000 questions; glos. 282 terms; 7 refs.; alf.; 21 x 14 cm; br.; *International Institute of Projectiology;* Rio de Janeiro, RJ; 1996; pages 52 to 251.

92. **Idem; *Nossa Evolução*** (Our Evolution); reviewer Tatiana Lopes; 170 p.; 15 chap.; 149 abbrev.; 17 emails; 1 photo; 1 microbiography; 162 questions; 162 answers; 13 websites; glos. 282 terms; 6 refs.; alf.; 21 x 14 cm; br.; 3rd Ed.; *Associação Internacional Editares;* Foz do Iguaçu, PR; 2010; pages 59 to 80.

93. **Idem; *Dicionário de Argumentos da Conscienciologia*** (Dictionary of Arguments of Conscientiology); reviewers: Team of Peer Reviewers of the Holocycle; 1.572 p.; 1 blog; 21 emails; 551 enus.; 1 scheme or consciential evolution; 18 photos; glos. 650 terms; 19 websites; alf.; 28,5 x 21,5 x 7 cm; enc.; *Associação Internacional Editares;* Foz do Iguaçu, PR; 2014; pages 107, 163, 198, 206, 208, 262, 314, 408, 464, 562, 638, 756, 783, 819, 877, 930, 950, 954, 959, 965, 971, 997, and 1,002.

94. **Idem; *Homo sapiens reurbanisatus;*** reviewers: Team of Peer Reviewers of the Holocycle; 1.584 p.; 24 sections; 479 chap.; 139 abbrev.; 12 emails; 597 enus.; 413 wordloans; 1 photo; 40 illus.; 1 microbiography; 25 tables; 4 websites; glos. 241 terms; 3 infographics; 102 films; 7.665 refs.; alf.; geo.; ono.; 29 x 21 x 7 cm; enc.; 3rd Ed. Free; *Associação Internacional do Centro de Altos Estudos da Conscienciologia* (CEAEC); Foz do Iguaçu, PR; 2004; pages 47, 214, 227, 229, 230, 245, 246, 275, 499, 602, 663, 674, 685 a 932, 1,038, and 1,122.

95. **Idem; *Homo sapiens pacificus*** reviewers: Team of Peer Reviewers of the Holocycle; 1.584 p.; 24 sections; 413 chap.; 403 abbrev.; 38 emails; 434 enus.; 484 wordloans; 1 photo; 37 illus.; 168 trivocabular megathosenes; 1 microbiography; 36 tables; 15 websites; glos. 241 terms; 25 pinacographies; 103 musicographies; 24 discographies; 20 scenographies; 240 films; 9.625 refs.; alf.; geo.; ono.; 29 x 21,5 x 7 cm; enc.; 3rd Ed. Free; *Associação Internacional do Centro de Altos Estudos da Conscienciologia (CEAEC);* & *Associação Internacional Editares;* Foz do Iguaçu, PR; 2007; pages 798, 908, and 946.

96. **Idem; *Léxico de Ortopensatas*** (Lexicon of Orthopensatas); reviewers Team of Peer Reviewers of the Holocycle; 2 Vols.; 1.800 p.; Vols. 1 e 2; 1 blog; 652 analogical concepts; 22 emails; 19 enus.; 1 scheme of consciential evolution; 17 photos; glos. 6.476 terms; 1.811 trivocabular megathosenes; 1 microbiography; 20.800 orthopensatas; 2 tables; 120 lexicographic techniques; 19 websites; 28,5 x 22 x 10 cm; enc.; *Associação Internacional Editares;* Foz do Iguaçu, PR; 2014; pages 55, 64, 108, 149, 156, 184, 187, 188, 192, 194, 228, 270, 286, 405, 503, 527, 616, 659, 670,

674, 713, 764, 910, 917, 922, 960, 970, 993, 1.047, 1,063; 1,068; 1,158, 1,159, 1,175, 1,364, 1,423, 1,465, 1,471, 1,472, 1,531, 1,575, 1,609 and 1,671.

97. **Idem;** *Manual da Dupla Evolutiva* (Manual of the Evolutionary Duo); reviewers Alexander Steiner; Cristiane Ferraro; & Graça Razera; 212 p.; 40 chap.; 17 emails; 88 enus.; 1 photo; 1 microbiography; 1 test; 2 websites; 16 refs.; alf.; 21 x 14 cm; br.; 2nd Ed.; *International Institute of Projectiology and Conscientiology* (IIPC); Rio de Janeiro, RJ; 1997; page 11.

98. **Idem;** *Manual da Proéxis* (Proexis Manual); reviewers Alexander Steiner; & Cristiane Ferraro; 172 p.; 40 chap.; 15 emails; 86 enus.; 1 photo; 1 microbiography; 2 websites; 17 refs.; alf.; 21 x 14 cm; br.; 2nd Ed. rev.; *International Institute of Projectiology and Conscientiology* (IIPC); 1998; Rio de Janeiro, RJ; pages 9, 17 to 19, 21, 56, and 116.

99. **Idem;** *Manual da Tenepes: Tarefa Energética Pessoal* (Penta Manual: Personal Energetic Task); reviewer Alexander Steiner; 142 p.; 34 chap.; 147 abbrev.; 1 *E-mail;* 52 enus.; 1 photo; 1 microbiography; 1 table; 1 test; glos. 282 terms; 5 refs.; alf.; 21 x 14 cm; br.; *International Institute of Projectiology;* Rio de Janeiro, RJ; 1995; pages 21 to 26.

100. **Idem;** *Manual de Redação da Conscienciologia* (Manual for Writing Conscientiology); reviewers Alexander Steiner; *et al.;* 276 p.; 15 sections; 150 chap.; 152 abbrev.; 23 emails; 54 enus.; 274 wordloans; 30 Portuguese idioms; 1 photo; 60 locutions of Spanish language; 85 trivocabular megathosenes; 1 microbiography; 30 researches; 6 techniques; 30 theories; 8 tests; 60 types of artifacts of knowledge; 60 voices of sughuman animals; 3 websites; glos. 300 terms; 609 refs.; 28 x 21 cm; br.; 2nf Ed. rev.; *Associação Internacional do Centro de Altos Estudos da Conscienciologia* (CEAEC); Foz do Iguaçu, PR; 2002; pages 13 to 204.

101. **Idem;** *Temas da Conscienciologia* (100 Themes of Conscientiology); reviewers Alexander Steiner; Cristiane Ferraro; & Graça Razera; 232 p.; 7 sections; 90 chap.; 10 diagnoses; 15 emails; 115 enus.; 1 photo; 1 microbiography; 10 researches; 30 conscientiometric tests; 2 tables; 2 websites; 16 refs.; alf.; ono.; 21 x 14 cm.; br.; *International Institute of Projectiology and Conscientiology* (IIPC); Rio de Janeiro, RJ; 1997; pages 160 and 161.

102. **Idem;** *Antepassado de Si Mesmo; Autorreflexão de 5 Horas; Cláusula Pétrea; Desperdício; Inteligência Evolutiva; Melin; Paradever; Parapolimatia; Parapsiquismo Intelectual; Partilha do Saber; Porão Consciencial; Prioridade; Riscomania; Tédio* (Ancestor of Oneself; 5-Hour Self-reflection; Fundamental Clause; Waste; Evolutionary Intelligence; Melin; Paraduty; Parapolymathy; Intellectual Parapsychism; Share of Knowledge; Consciential Basement; Priority: Riskmania; Boredom); *verbets*; In: **Vieira;** Waldo; Org.; ***Encyclopaedia of Conscientiology;*** electronic; CD-ROM; 2.498 *verbets*; 11.034 p.; 234 specialities; glos. 2.498 entries (*verbets*); 192 microbiographies; 147 tables; 191 verbetographers; 8th Ed. Digital; version 8.00; *Associação Internacional Editares;* & *Associação do Centro de Altos Estudos da Conscienciologia* (CEAEC); Foz do Iguaçu, PR; 2013; pages 650 to 655, 2,011 to 2,014, 2,801 to 2,804, 3,977 to 3,980, 6,108 to 6,113, 7,202 to 7,205, 7,943 to 7,946, 8,111 to 8,113, 8,138 to 8,141, 8,258 to 8,261; 8,568 to 8,571, 8,847 to 8,850, 9,614 to 9,616, and 10,411 to 10,413.

103. **Wood,** John; ***Saí da Microsoft para Mudar o Mundo*** *(Leaving Microsoft to Change the World);* reviewers José Tedin Pinto; Luis Américo Costa; & Tereza da Rocha; transl. Mário Molina; 240 p.; 24 chap.; 20 x 13 cm; br.; *Sextante;* Rio de Janeiro, RJ; 2007; pages 63 to 201.

104. **Xausa,** Izar; ***A Psicologia do Sentido da Vida*** (The Psychology of the Meaning of Life); 256 p.; 5 chap.; 175 refs.; 21 x 13,5 cm; br.; *Vozes;* Petrópolis, RJ; 1986; pages 13 to 210.

WEBGRAPHY (SPECIFIC):

1.   **Robson,** David; ***O Surpreendente Lado Ruim de Ser Inteligente*** (The Surprising Bad Side to Being Intelligent); available at: http://www.bbc.com/portuguese/noticias/2015/04/150417_vert_fut_lado_ruim_inteligencia_ml; accessed on 14.05.16.

2.   **United Nations;** *Department of Economic and Social Affairs, Population Division (2015). World Population Prospects: The 2015 Revision, Key Findings and Advance Tables, Working Paper;* No. ESA/P/WP.241; New York, 2015; available at: <http://esa.un.org/unpd/wpp/Publications/Files/Key_Findings_WPP_2015.pdf>; accessed on: 10.05.16.

Prescription of Anti-self-wastage Encyclopaedia Verbets

Definition. Nader (1951–) defines the *prescription of verbets, or encyclopaedic entries,* as a set of prescriptions constituted by a group of verbets in the *Encyclopaedia of Conscientiology* to promote the theorical self-research of a conscin recently arrived in the universe of the conscientiological neoscience, aiming at the remission of personal pathologies or the qualification of potentialities (See **Nader;** Rosa; *Encyclopaedic-verbets prescription; verbet;* In: **Vieira,** Waldo; Org.; *Encyclopaedia of Conscientiology;* defended at the *CEAEC Tertuliarium,* Foz do Iguaçu, PR, on: 16.11.2016).

Reference. The unprecedented proposal of organizing an *Encyclopaedia-verbet prescription* was made by Dr Waldo Vieira on 02.09.2008, during the daily Conscientiological *Tertulia* at the CEAEC, Foz do Iguaçu, PR, Brazil.

Prescriptiology. When a pathology or dysfunction is diagnosed, there is often an indication of therapeutics that can resolve the problem. Following the reader will find a prescription of 100 verbets, or entries, from the *Encyclopaedia of Conscientiology,* from different verbetographers, *listed in alphabetic order,* this author wishes to suggest destined to help in the process of remission of the *Self-wastage Syndrome,* and as a prophylaxis (prevention) of this nosological condition:

01. **Abundance** (Intraphysicology; Neutral).

02. **Opportunity to live** (Proexology; Homeostatic).

03. **Antiprocrastination** (Self-discernmentology; Homeostatic).

04. **Anti-self-doldrumology** (Gesconology; Homeostatic).

05. **Anti-utilitarian** (Self-discernmentology; Nosographic).

06. **Appreciation for self-lucidity** (Self-lucidology; Homeostatic).

07. **Approaching an opportunity** (Self-lucidology; Homeostatic).

08. **Ascendant self-familiarity** (Self-conviviology; Homeostatic).

09. **Avoidable resource** (Recexiology; Homeostatic).

10. **Avoidance of self-obsolescence** (Antiwastology; Homeostatic).

11. **Avoidance of self-wastage** (Self-proexology; Homeostatic).

12. **Bonus of No** (Crescendology; Neutral).

13. **Boredom** (Parapathology; Nosographic).

14. **Career non-ambition** (Proexology; Homeostatic).

15. **Choice of evolutionary route** (Evolutiology; Homeostatic).

16. **Consciential bond** (Conscientiometrology; Neutral).

17. *Consciential dispersion syndrome* (Antievolutiology; Nosographic).

18. **Consciential self-organization** (Self-organizatiology; Neutral).

19. **Consciential waste** (Intraphysicology; Nosographic).

20. **Criteriology** (Self-discernmentology; Homeostatic).

21. **Critical self-decision** (Self-decidology; Neutral).

22. **Daily antidispersivity** (Routinology; Neutral).

23. **Daily existential completism** (Self-proexology; Homeostatic).

24. **Decennial self-determination** (Self-determinology; Homeostatic).

25. **Decisive anorexia** (Decidology; Nosographic).

26. **Dedramatization** (Self-discernmentology; Homeostatic).

27. **Destagnation of an intermissivist** (Self-prioriology; Homeostatic).

28. **Deviationism** (Proexology; Nosographic).

29. **Dormant strongtrait** (Strongtraitology; Nosographic).

30. **Evolutionary confrontation** (Proexology; Homeostatic).

31. **Evolutionary choice** (Experimentology; Homeostatic).

32. **Evolutionary potentialization** (Evolutiology; Homeostatic).

33. **Evolutionary quotient** (Conscientiometrology; Neutral).

34. **Evolutionary relevance** (Self-discernmentology; Homeostatic).

35. **Existential input** (Proexology; Homeostatic).

36. **Existential self-management** (Self-proexology; Neutral).

37. **Existential value** (Paraxiology; Neutral).

38. **Existential void** (Proexology; Nosographic).

39. **Final existential goal** (Proexology; Homeostatic).

40. **Good use of time** (Self-proexology; Homeostatic).

41. **Idle capacity in proexis** (Proexometricology; Nosographic).

42. **Intellectual dispersion** (Dispersiology; Nosographic).

43. **Intention of change** (Self-proexology; Neutral).

44. ***Interaction Abundanceology-Wastology*** (Discernmentology; Nosographic).

45. ***Interaction of contributions*** (Proexology; Homeostatic).

46. **Intermissivist handbook** (Proexology; Homeostatic).

47. **Inventariology** (Proexology; Homeostatic).

48. ***Law of the proexis*** (Proexology; Homeostatic).

49. **Line of the opening** (Self-proexology; Homeostatic).

50. **Lucidology** (Self-conscientiology; Homeostatic).

51. **Mathematic life** (Holomaturology; Neutral).

52. **Megafocal direction** (Proexology; Neutral).

53. **Megaomission** (Self-discernmentology; Nosographic).

54. **Millimetric planning** (Self-proexology; Homeostatic).

55. **Omnifrivolity** (Parapathology; Nosographic).

56. **Onus of difference** (Uniquology; Neutral).

57. *Paradox of self-deception* (Self-lucidology; Neutral).

58. **Personal priorities handbook** (Proexology; Homeostatic).

59. **Prevention of haste** (Self-prioriology; Homeostatic).

60. *Principle of compulsory priority* (Holomaturology; Homeostatic).

61. **Prioriology** (Evolutiology; Neutral).

62. **Prioritization of proexis** (Proexology; Homeostatic).

63. **Priority** (Self-evolutiology; Neutral).

64. **Priority objective** (Self-discernmentology; Homeostatic).

65. **Priority rank** (Self-experimentology; Homeostatic).

66. **Priority resolution** (Self-prioriology; Homeostatic).

67. **Proevolutionary reprimand** (Interassistantiology; Homeostatic).

68. **Proexological marathon** (Proexology; Homeostatic).

69. **Proexological priority** (Self-proexology; Homeostatic).

70. **Proexological protagonism** (Proexology; Homeostatic).

71. **Proexological self-lucidity** (Proexology; Homeostatic).

72. **Proexopathy** (Proexopathology; Nosographic)

73. **Prudent audacity** (Self-discernmentology; Homeostatic).

74. **Quinquagenarian self-audit** (Self-proexogramology; Neutral).

75. **Relevant approach** (Self-prioriology; Homeostatic).

76. **Resolute intelligence** (Self-discernmentology; Homeostatic).

77. **Reciprocatiology** (Proexology; Homeostatic).

78. *Scale of evolutionary priorities* (Evolutiology; Homeostatic).

79. **Scarce good** (Self-prioriology; Neutral).

80. **Self-critical sense** (Self-maturology; Homeostatic).

81. **Self-deprioritization** (Self-discernmentology; Nosographic).

82. **Self-evolutionary turning** (Self-evolutiology; Homeostatic).

83. **Self-experience of priorities** (Self-prioriology; Homeostatic).

84. **Self-prioriology** (Self-discernmentology; Neutral).

85. **Self-thosenic amplitude** (Proexology; Homeostatic).

86. *Self-wastage syndrome* (Parapathology; Nosographic).

87. **Sense of evolutionary usefulness** (Evolutiology; Homeostatic).

88. **Sense of existential orientation** (Evolutiology; Homeostatic).

89. **Strengthening setback** (Intraphysicology; Homeostatic).

90. **Top of self-sufficiency** (Self-maturology; Homeostatic).

91. *Trinomial motivation-work-leisure technique* (Intraphysicology; Neutral).

92. *Trinomial priority–challenge–self-overcoming* (Recexiology; Homeostatic).

93. **Trivialization of self-strongtraits** (Strongtraitology; Nosographic).

94. *Underestimation syndrome* (Parapathology; Nosographic).

95. **Unused longevity** (Wastology; Nosographic).

96. **Verbet prescription** (Claritaskology; Neutral).

97. **Wastage** (Ecology; Nosographic).

98. **Wasted precocity** (Wastology; Nosographic).

99. **Window of opportunity** (Evolutiology; Homeostatic).

100. **Writing strongtrait** (Strongtraitology; Homeostatic).

Geographic Index

A

Africa
    South 77
    West 45
Ancient Greece 147
Athens 30

C

Cambodia 77
Canada 102
Cognopolis 148

E

England 27, 29
Europe 28

F

France 28

I

India 77

L

Laos 77

N

Nepal 77

P

Paris 28

S

Sri-Lanka 77

U

United States 25

V

Vietnam 77

Onomastic Index

W

Remissive Index

Conscientiocentric Institutions (Ics)

CIs. The Conscientiocentric Institutions – CIs – are organizations whose purposes, methodologies of work and organizational models are based in the *Consciential Paradigm*. The main activity of the CIs is to support the evolution of the consciousnesses through the *clarifying task* guided by the *cutting edge relative truths*, found in researches in the field of the Science Conscientiology and its specialties.

Volunteer. Every Conscientiocentric Institution is an independent association, of private character, non-profit and maintained predominantly by volunteer work of teachers, researchers, administrators and professionals of several areas.

CCCI. The set of Conscientiocentric Institutions and Conscientiology's volunteers in the planet composes the *International Cosmoethical Conscientiological Community* which currently consists of 25 CIs.

AIEC – Associação Internacional para Expansão da Conscienciologia (International Association for Expansion of Conscientiology)

Foundation: 22/04/2005

Head office: Av. Felipe Wandscheer, 6.200, sala 111, Cognópolis Foz do Iguaçu, Paraná, Brasil, CEP: 85856-530

Phone: +55 (45) 2102-1411

Website: www.worldaiec.org

Email: aiec.comunicacao@gmail.com

Campus Discernimentum: Av. Felipe Wandscheer, 6.200, sala 201 Cognópolis, Foz do Iguaçu, Paraná, Brasil, CEP: 85856-530

Phone: +55 (45) 2102-1400

Email: contato@discernimentum.org

APEX – Associação Internacional da Programação Existencial (Intenational Association of Existential Program)

Foundation: 20/02/2007

Head office: Rua da Cosmoética, 1.635, Cognópolis, Caixa Postal 921, Centro Foz do Iguaçu, Paraná, Brasil, CEP: 85853-755

Phone: +55 (45) 3525-2652 – Fax: +55 (45) 3525-5511

Website: www.apexinternacional.org

Email: contato@apexinternacional.org

ARACÊ – Associação Internacional para Evolução da Consciência (International Association for Consciousness Evolution)

    Foundation: 14/04/2001

    Campus **ARACÊ:** Rota do Conhecimento, Km 7, acesso pela BR-262 Km 87, Distrito de Arace, Domingos Martins, Espírito Santo, Brasil

    Mailing address: Caixa Postal 110, Pedra Azul Domingos Martins, Espírito Santo, Brasil CEP: 29278-000

    Phone: +55 (27) 9739-2400

    Website: www.arace.org

    Email: associacao@arace.org

ASSINVÉXIS – Associação Internacional de Inversão Existencial (International Association of Existential Inversion)

    Foundation: 22/07/2004

    Invexology *Campus*: Av. Maria Bubiak, 1.100, Cognópolis Foz do Iguaçu, Paraná, Brasil CEP: 85853-728

    Phone: +55 (45) 3525-0913

    Website: www.assinvexis.org

    Email: contato@assinvexis.org

ASSIPEC – Associação Internacional de Pesquisas da Conscienciologia (International Association of Research in Conscientiology)

    Foundation: CI officially presented in 14/08/2011

    Head office: Rua XV de Novembro, 1.681, Vila Municipal Jundiaí, Sao Paulo, Brasil CEP: 13201-006

    Phone: +55 (11) 4521-8541

    Website: www.assipec.org

    Email: assipec@assipec.org

ASSIPI – Associação Internacional de Parapsiquismo Interassistencial (International Association of Interassistential Parapsychism)

    Foundation: 29/12/2011

    Head office: Av. Felipe Wandscheer, 6.200, sala 212, Cognópolis, Foz do Iguaçu, Paraná, Brasil CEP: 85856-530

    Phone: +55 (11) 2102-1421 – VOIP: +55 (45) 4053-9818

    Website: www.assipi.org

    Email: assipi@assipi.com

CEAEC – Associação Internacional do Centro de Altos Estudos da Conscienciologia (International Association of the Center for Advanced Studies of Conscientiology)

Foundation: 15/07/1995
Head office: Rua da Cosmoética, 1.635, Cognópolis, Caixa Postal 921, Centro Foz do Iguaçu, Paraná, Brasil CEP: 85853-755
Phone: +55 (45) 3525-2652 – Fax:+55 (45) 3525-5511
Website: www.ceaec.org
Email: ceaec@ceaec.org

COMUNICONS – Associação Internacional de Comunicação Conscienciológica (International Association of Conscientiological Communication)

Foundation: 24/07/2005
Head office: Av. Felipe Wandscheer, 6.200, sala 206, Cognópolis Foz do Iguaçu, Paraná, Brasil CEP: 85856-530
Phone: +55 (45) 2102-1409
Website: www.comunicons.org.br
Email: comunicons@comunicons.org

CONSCIUS – Associação Internacional de Conscienciometria Interassistencial (International Association of Interassistantial Conscientiometry)

Foundation: 24/02/2006
Head office: Av. Felipe Wandscheer, 6.200, casa 352, Cognópolis Foz do Iguaçu, Paraná, Brasil CEP: 85856-530
Phone: +55 (45) 2102-1460
Website: www.conscius.org.br
Email: conscius@conscius.org.br

CONSECUTIVUS – Associação Internacional de Pesquisas Seriexológicas e Holobiográficas (International Association of Seriexologic and Holobiographic Research)

Foundation: 14/12/2014
Head office: Av. Felipe Wandscheer, 6.200, Casa 351, Cognópolis Foz do Iguaçu, Paraná, Brasil CEP: 85851-579
Phone: +55 (45) 9807-1320
Website: www.consecutivus.com.br
Email: consecutivus@consecutivus.com.br 226

COSMOETHOS – ASSOCIAÇÃO INTERNACIONAL DE COSMOETICOLOGIA (INTERNATIONAL ASSOCIATION OF COSMOETHICOLOGY)

Foundation: 03/10/2015

Head office: Av. Felipe Wandscheer, 6.200, Sala 104, *Cosmoethicarium* Cognópolis Foz do Iguaçu, Paraná, Brasil CEP: 85851-579

Phone: +55 (45) 9807-1320

Website: www.cosmoethos.org.br

Email: contato@cosmoethos.com.br

ECTOLAB – ASSOCIAÇÃO INTERNACIONAL DE PESQUISA LABORATORIAL EM ECTOPLASMIA E PARACIRURGIA (INTERNATIONAL ASSOCIATION OF LABORATORIAL RESEARCH IN ECTOPLASMY AND PARASURGERY)

Foundation: 14/07/2013

Head office: Avenida Felipe Wandscheer, 6.200, sala 105, Cognópolis Foz do Iguaçu, PR, Brasil CEP: 85856-630 **Telefone:** +55 (45) 2102-1427

Website: www.ectolab.org

Email: ectolab@ectolab.org

EDITARES – ASSOCIAÇÃO INTERNACIONAL EDITARES (INTERNATIONAL ASSOCIATION EDITARES)

Foundation: 23/10/2004

Head office: Av. Felipe Wandscheer, 6.200, sala 107, Cognópolis Foz do Iguaçu, Paraná, Brasil CEP: 85856-530

Phone: +55 (45) 2102-1407

Website: www.editares.org.br **Shopcons:** www.shopcons.com.br (portal de compra de livros)

Email: editares@editares.org

ENCYCLOSSAPIENS – ASSOCIAÇÃO INTERNACIONAL DE ENCICLOPEDIOLOGIA CONSCIENCIOLÓGICA (INTERNATIONAL ASSOCIATION OF CONSCIENTIOLOGICAL ENCYCLOPEDIOLOGY)

Foundation: 21/12/2013

Head office: Rua da Cosmoética, 1.635, Cognópolis, Foz do Iguaçu, Paraná, Brasil CEP: 85853-755, Caixa Postal 921

Phone: +55 (45) 3525-2652 – Fax: +55 (45) 3525-5511

Website: www.encyclossapiens.org

Email: contato@encyclossapiens.org

EVOLUCIN – Associação Internacional de Conscienciologia para Infância (International Association of Conscientiology for Youth)
Foundation: 09/07/2006
Head office: Av. Felipe Wandscheer, 6.200, sala 102, Cognópolis Foz do Iguaçu, Paraná, Brasil, CEP: 85856-530
Phone: +55 (45) 9909-6129
Website: www.evolucin.org
Email: evolucin@gmail.com

IC TENEPES – Associação Internacional de Tenepessologia (International Association of Pentology)
Foundation: 11/06/2016
Head office: Felipe Wandscheer 6.200, Sala 205, Cognópolis Foz do Iguaçu, Paraná, Brasil, CEP: 85856-530
Phone: +55 (45) 9131-2855
Website: www.ictenepes.org

INTERPARES – Associação Internacional de Aportes Interassistenciais (International Association of Interassistential Intakes)
Foundation: 15/05/2016
Head office: Rua da Cosmoética, 1635, sala 11, Cognópolis Foz do Iguaçu, Paraná, Brasil, CEP: 85853-755
Phone: +55 (45) 3525-2652
Website: www.interpares.org.br
Email: aslascani@yahoo.com.br

IIPC – Instituto Internacional de Projeciologia e Conscienciologia (International Institute of Projectiology and Conscientiology)
Foundation: 16/01/1988
Head office: Av. Felipe Wandscheer, 6.200, sala 103, Cognópolis Foz do Iguaçu, Paraná, Brasil, CEP: 85856-530
Phone: +55 (45) 2102-1448
Website:: www.iipc.org.br
Email: iipc@iipc.org.br
IIPC *Research Campus*: Estrada do Universalismo, 1.177 Sampaio Correa, Saquarema, Rio de Janeiro, Brasil, CEP: 28997-970
Phone: +55 (22) 2654-1186
Email: campussaquarema@iipc.org

INTERCAMPI – ASSOCIAÇÃO INTERNACIONAL DOS *CAMPI* DE PESQUISAS DA CONSCIENCIOLOGIA (INTERNATIONAL ASSOCIATION OF THE CAMPI OF RESEARCH IN CONSCIENTIOLOGY)

> Foundation: 23/07/2005
> Head office: Av. Antonio Basílio, 3006, sala 602, Lagoa Nova Natal, Rio Grande do Norte, CEP: 59056-005
> Phone: +55 (84) 3211-3126
> Website: www.intercampi.org
> Email: intercampi@intercampi.org

JURISCONS – ASSOCIAÇÃO INTERNACIONAL DE PARADIREITOLOGIA (INTERNATIONAL ASSOCIATION OF PARALAWOLOGY)

> Foundation: 25/04/2015
> Head office: Av. Felipe Wandscheer, 6.200, sala 350 A, Cognópolis Foz do Iguaçu, Paraná, Brasil, CEP: 85856-530
> Website: www.juriscons.org
> Email: juriscons@juriscons.org

OIC – ORGANIZAÇÃO INTERNACIONAL DE CONSCIENCIOTERAPIA (INTERNATIONAL ORGANIZATION OF CONSCIENTIOTHERAPY)

> Foundation: 06/09/2003
> *Campus* OIC: Av. Felipe Wandscheer, 5.935, Cognópolis Foz do Iguaçu, Paraná, Brasil, CEP: 85856-530
> Phone: +55 (45) 3025-1404 / 2102-1402
> Website: www.oic.org.br
> Email: aco@oic.org.br

ORTHOCOGNITIVUS – ASSOCIAÇÃO INTERNACIONAL PARA IMPLANTAÇÃO DA COGNÓPOLIS EM SC (INTERNATIONAL ASSOCIATION FOR THE IMPLEMENTATION OF COGNOPOLIS IN SC)

> Foundation: 18/05/2018
> Head office: Av. Mal. Castelo Branco, 65, Sala 1111, Torre II, Campinas, São José, Santa Catarina, Brasil, CEP: 88101-020
> Phone: +55 (48) 99845-9931
> Website: www.cognopolis-sc.org
> Email: contato@cognopolis-sc.org

REAPRENDENTIA – Associação Internacional de Parapedagogia e Reeducação Consciencial (International Association of Parapedagogy and Consciential Reeducation)

> **Foundation:** 21/10/2007
> **Head office:** Av. Felipe Wandscheer, 6.560, Cognópolis Foz do Iguaçu, Paraná, Brasil, CEP: 85853-755 Caixa Postal 921, Centro
> **Phone:** +55 (45) 3525-2652 – Fax: +55 (45) 3525-5511
> **Website:** www.reaprendentia.org
> **Email:** contato@reaprendentia.org.br

UNICIN – União das Instituições Conscienciocêntricas Internacionais (Union of the International Conscientiocentric Institutions)

> **Foundation:** 22/01/2005
> **Head office:** Av. Felipe Wandscheer, 6.200, sala 105, Cognópolis Foz do Iguaçu, Paraná, Brasil, CEP: 85856-530
> **Phone:** +55 (45) 2102-1405
> **Website:** www.unicin.org
> **Email:** unicin@unicin.org

UNIESCON – União Internacional de Escritores da Conscienciologia (Union of Writers of Conscientiology)

> **Foundation:** 23/11/2008
> **Head office:** Rua da Cosmoética, 1.635, Cognópolis Foz do Iguaçu, Paraná, Brasil, CEP: 85853-755
> **Phone:** +55 (45) 3525-2652

Editares' Publications

English

AUTHOR	TITLE
Alessandra Nascimento / Felix Wong (Orgs.)	CONSCIENTIOLOGY IS NEWS: PROJECTIOLOGY
Jayme Pereira	BARBARAH VISITS A STAR
Marcelo da Luz	WHERE DOES RELIGION END?
Waldo Vieira	700 CONSCIENTIOLOGY EXPERIMENTS
	CONSCIENTIOGRAM
	OUR EVOLUTION
	PENTA MANUAL
	PROEXIS MANUAL
	PROJECTIOLOGY – A PANORAMA OF EXPERIENCES OF THE CONSCIOUSNESS OUTSIDE THE HUMAN BODY
	PROJECTIONS OF THE CONSCIOUSNESS

Spanish

AUTHOR	TITLE
Alessandra Nascimento / Felix Wong (Orgs.)	CONCIENCIOLOGÍA ES NOTICIA: PROYECCIOLOGÍA
Gloria Thiago	VIVIENDO EN MULTIPLES DIMENSIONES
Malu Balona	SÍNDROME DEL EXTRANJERO
Maximiliano Haymann	SÍNDROME DEL OSTRACISMO
Miguel Cirera	EVOLUCIÓN DE LA INTELIGENCIA PARAPSÍQUICA
Rosemary Salles	CONCIENCIA EN REVOLUCIÓN
Waldo Vieira	CONSCIENCIOGRAMA
	NUESTRA EVOLUCIÓN
	MANUAL DE LA TENEPER
	MANUAL DE LA PROEXIS
	PROYECCIONES DE LA CONCIENCIA

German

AUTHOR	TITLE
Jayme Pereira	BARBARAH FLIEGT ZUM STERN

Portuguese

AUTOR	TÍTULO
Adriana Kauati	SÍNDROME DO IMPOSTOR
Adriana Lopes	SENSOS EVOLUTIVOS E CONTRASSENSOS REGRESSIVOS
Alessandra Nascimento / Felix Wong (Orgs.)	CONSCIENCIOLOGIA É NOTÍCIA – PROJECIOLOGIA
Alexandre Nonato	JK E OS BASTIDORES DA CONSTRUÇÃO DE BRASÍLIA
Alexandre Nonato et. al.	ACOPLAMENTO ENERGÉTICO
Alexandre Nonato et. al.	INVERSÃO EXISTENCIAL
Alexandre Zaslavsky (editor).	INTERPARADIGMAS N.1 – Princípio da Descrença INTERPARADIGMAS N.2 – Parapercepciologia INTERPARADIGMAS N.3 – Pesquisa da Autoconsciência
Aline Niemeyer	MEGAPENSENES TRIVOCABULARES DA INTERASSISTENCIALIDADE
Aline Niemeyer / Lilian Zolet	TÉCNICAS BIOENERGÉTICAS PARA CRIANÇAS
Almir Justi, Amin Lascani e Dayane Rossa	COMPETÊNCIAS PARAPSÍQUICAS
Alzemiro Rufino de Matos	VIDA: OPORTUNIDADE DE APRENDER
Alzira Gesing	INTENÇÃO
Ana Seno	COMUNICAÇÃO EVOLUTIVA
Anália Rosário Lopes / Myriam Sanchez / Rita Sawaya	DICIONÁRIO DE TECAS DA HOLOTECOLOGIA
Antonio Pitaguari / Marina Thomaz	REDAÇÃO E ESTILÍSTICA CONSCIENCIOLÓGICA
Arlindo Alcadipani	ITINERÁRIO EVOLUTIVO DE UM RECICLANTE
Bárbara Ceotto	DIÁRIO DE AUTOCURA
Cesar Machado	ANTIVITIMIZAÇÃO
Cesar Machado	PROATIVIDADE EVOLUTIVA
Cesar Machado / Stéfani Sabetzki	HUMANIZAÇÃO PARAPSÍQUICA NA UTI

Autor	Obra
Cirleine Couto	CONTRAPONTOS DO PARAPSIQUISMO
	INTELIGÊNCIA EVOLUTIVA COTIDIANA
Dalva Morem	SEMPRE É TEMPO
Dayane Rossa	OPORTUNIDADE DE VIVER
Débora Klippel	O PEQUENO PESQUISADOR: MULTIDIMENSIONALIDADE
Dulce Daou	AUTOCONSCIÊNCIA E MULTIDIMENSIONALIDADE
	VONTADE: CONSCIÊNCIA INTEIRA
Eduardo Martins	HIGIENE CONSCIENCIAL
Eliana Manfroi	ANTIDESPERDÍCIO CONSCIENCIAL
Fernando R. Sivelli / Marineide C. Gregório	AUTOEXPERIMENTOGRAFIA PROJECIOLÓGICA
Flavia Rogick	MUDAR OU MUDAR
	CONSCiÊNCIA CENTRADA NA ASSISTÊNCIA
Flavio Amado	TEÁTICAS DA TENEPES
Flávio Buononato	ANUÁRIO DA CONSCIENCIOLOGIA 2012
	ANUÁRIO DA CONSCIENCIOLOGIA 2013
	FATOS E PARAFATOS DA COGNÓPOLIS FOZ DO IGUAÇU
Flávio Monteiro e Pedro Marcelino	CONS – COMPREENDENDO NOSSA EVOLUÇÃO
Graça Razera	HIPERATIVIDADE EFICAZ
Guilherme Kunz	MANUAL DO MATERPENSENE
Isabel Manfroi	O EMPREENDEDORISMO REURBANIZADOR DE HÉRCULES GALLÓ E WALDO VIEIRA
Jacqueline Nahas / Pedro Fernandes	*HOMO LEXICOGRAPHUS*
Jayme Pereira	BÁRBARAH VAI À ESTRELA
	Princípios do Estado Mundial Cosmoético
João Aurélio / Kátia Arakaki	COGNÓPOLIS FOZ: UM LUGAR PARA SE VIVER
João Paulo Costa / Dayane Rossa	MANUAL DA CONSCIN-COBAIA
Jovilde Montagna	VIVÊNCIAS PARAPSÍQUICAS DE UMA PEDIATRA
Julieta Mendonça	MANUAL DO TEXTO DISSERTATIVO
Julio Almeida	QUALIFICAÇÃO AUTORAL
	QUALIFICAÇÕES DA CONSCIÊNCIA
Kátia Arakaki	ANTIBAGULHISMO ENERGÉTICO – MANUAL
	VIAGENS INTERNACIONAIS
Laura Sánchez	LASTANOSA: MEMÓRIA E HISTÓRIA DO INTELECTUAL E HOLOTECÁRIO DO SÉCULO XVII
Lilian Zolet	PARAPSIQUISMO NA INFÂNCIA

Autor	Obra
Lilian Zolet / Flávio Buononato	MANUAL DO *ACOPLAMENTARIUM*
Lilian Zolet / Guilherme Kunz	*ACOPLAMENTARIUM:* PRIMEIRA DÉCADA
Lourdes Pinheiro / Felipe Araújo	DICIONÁRIO DE VERBOS CONJUGADOS DA LÍNGUA PORTUGUESA
Luciana Lavôr (Org.)	I NOITE DE GALA MNEMÔNICA
Luciano Vicenzi	CORAGEM PARA EVOLUIR
Lucy Lutfi	VOLTEI PARA CONTAR
Luiz Bonassi	PARADOXOS
Mabel Teles	PROFILAXIA DAS MANIPULAÇÕES CONSCIENCIAIS
Mabel Teles	ZÉFIRO
Málu Balona	AUTOCURA ATRAVÉS DA RECONCILIAÇÃO
Málu Balona	SÍNDROME DO ESTRANGEIRO
Marcelo da Luz	ONDE A RELIGIÃO TERMINA?
Maria Helena Lagrota	MINHAS QUATRO ESTAÇÕES
Maria Thereza Lacerda	A PEDRA DO CAMINHO
Marilza Andrade	PROJEÇÕES ASSISTENCIAIS
Marina Thomaz / Antonio Pitaguari (Orgs.)	TENEPES: ASSISTÊNCIA INTERDIMENSIONAL LÚCIDA
Marta Ramiro	MANUAL DA TÉCNICA DA RECÉXIS
Maximiliano Haymann	PRESCRIÇÕES PARA O AUTODESASSÉDIO
Maximiliano Haymann	SÍNDROME DO OSTRACISMO
Moacir Gonçalves / Rosemary Salles	DINÂMICAS PARAPSÍQUICAS
Osmar Ramos Filho	CRISTO ESPERA POR TI (Edição Comentada)
Paulo Mello	EVOLUTIVIDADE PLANEJADA
Phelipe Mansur	EMPREENDEDORISMO EVOLUTIVO
Reinalda Fritzen	CAMINHOS DE AUTOSSUPERAÇÃO
Roberto Leimig	VIDAS DE NATURALISTA
Rodrigo Medeiros	CLARIVIDÊNCIA
Rosa Nader	MANUAL DE VERBETOGRAFIA
Roseli Oliveira	DICIONÁRIO DE EUFEMISMOS DA LÍNGUA PORTUGUESA
Rosemary Salles	CONSCIÊNCIA EM REVOLUÇÃO
Sandra Tornieri	MAPEAMENTO DA SINALÉTICA ENERGÉTICA PARAPSÍQUICA
Silda Dries	TEORIA E PRÁTICA DA EXPERIÊNCIA FORA DO CORPO
Tathiana Mota	CURSO INTERMISSIVO
Tatiana Lopes	DESENVOLVIMENTO DA PROJETABILIDADE LÚCIDA

Tony Musskopf	AUTENTICIDADE CONSCIENCIAL
Vera Hoffmann	SEM MEDO DA MORTE
Vera Tanuri	PERDÃO
Wagner Alegretti	RETROCOGNIÇÕES
Waldo Vieira	500 VERBETÓGRAFOS DA ENCICLOPÉDIA DA CONSCIENCIOLOGIA
	700 EXPERIMENTOS DA CONSCIENCIOLOGIA
	DICIONÁRIO DE ARGUMENTOS DA CONSCIENCIOLOGIA
	Dicionário de Neologismos da Conscienciologia
	ENCICLOPÉDIA DA CONSCIENCIOLOGIA
	HOMO SAPIENS PACIFICUS
	HOMO SAPIENS REURBANISATUS
	LÉXICO DE ORTOPENSATAS
	MANUAL DA DUPLA EVOLUTIVA
	MANUAL DA PROÉXIS
	MANUAL DA TENEPES
	MANUAL DOS MEGAPENSENES TRIVOCABULARES
	NOSSA EVOLUÇÃO
	O QUE É A CONSCIENCIOLOGIA
	PROJECIOLOGIA
	PROJEÇÕES DA CONSCIÊNCIA

Where to buy:

www.shopcons.com.br

www.iipc.org/loja

www.editares.org

Eliana Manfroi was born in 1962 in Caxias do Sul, RS, Brazil, a descendant of Italian immigrants. She has degrees in Journalism and Psychology, as well as a Masters in Clinical Psychology. She worked in newspapers, public health, and university teaching.

Volunteer and teacher of Conscientiology since 1998, she currently resides in the *Cognopolis* borough of Foz do Iguaçu, PR, Brazil. She has of late been focusing on the expansion and dissemination of the *corpus* of ideas and practices proposed under the conscientual paradigm, notably through the writing and revision of entries, also known as *verbets,* for the *Enciyclopaedia of Conscientiology,* at ENCYCLOSSAPIENS, the *Internacional Association of Conscientiologic Encyclopaediology,* and through teaching and researching at the CEAEC – *Centre for the Higher Studies of Conscientiology.*

1. Research Area:

This book investigates themes in

Self-discernmentology,

a sub-discipline of Conscientiology.

Principle of Disbelief:

Do not belive anything, not even

in the information presented in this book.

It is best to carry out personal

experiments on the topics.